ALBANIA

WESTVIEW PROFILES · NATIONS OF CONTEMPORARY EASTERN EUROPE

Albania: A Socialist Maverick, Elez Biberaj

Poland: Socialist State, Rebellious Nation, Ray Taras

The German Democratic Republic: The Search for Identity, Henry Krisch

FORTHCOMING

Yugoslavia: Tradition and Change in a Multiethnic State, Lenard J. Cohen

Bulgaria: A Modernizing Balkan Autocracy, William A. Welsh

ALBANIA

A Socialist Maverick

Elez Biberaj

Westview Press

BOULDER, SAN FRANCISCO, & OXFORD

Westview Profiles/Nations of Contemporary Eastern Europe

Cover illustration: Two-headed eagle as depicted on the Albanian flag.

Copyright © 1990 by Westview Press, Inc.

Published in 1990 in the United States of America by Westview Press, Inc., 5500 Central Avenue, Boulder, Colorado 80301, and in the United Kingdom by Westview Press, Inc., 36 Lonsdale Road, Summertown, Oxford OX2 7EW

Library of Congress Cataloging-in-Publication Data
Biberaj, Elez.
  Albania.
  (Westview profiles. Nations of contemporary Eastern
Europe)
  Bibliography: p.
  Includes index.
  1. Albania—History—1944–   . I. Title.
II. Series: Nations of contemporary Eastern Europe.
DR977.B53 1990 949.6′503   87-14613
ISBN 0-8133-0513-6

Printed and bound in the United States of America

The paper used in this publication meets the requirements
of the American National Standard for Permanence of Paper
for Printed Library Materials Z39.48-1984.

10   9   8   7   6   5   4   3   2   1

Contents

List of Tables and Illustrations vii

1 The Land and the People 1

Geographical Setting, 3
The People, 5
Early History, 10
National Awakening and Independence, 12

2 Albania Under Hoxha 15

The Road to Power, 16
Political Developments, 1945–1960, 19
Albania's Road to Self-Assertion, 24
Domestic Politics, 28

3 From Hoxha to Alia 33

Mehmet Shehu's Demise, 33
Alia's Accession to Power, 38
Alia: Charting a New Course, 42

4 Government and Politics 51

The Party, 53
The State, 58
Mass Organizations, 61
Conclusion, 64

5 The Economy 67

Economic Achievements and Difficulties, 67

The Perils of Central Planning, 72
Prospects for Economic Reform, 74
Conclusion, 82

6   Foreign Policy   85

Albania's Opening Up in the Early 1980s, 87
Alia: Foreign Policy Pragmatism, 90
Relations with Neighbors, 93
Relations with the West, 100
Relations with the Soviet Bloc, 103
Conclusion, 104

7   The Albanians in Yugoslavia   107

The Roots of the Problem, 112
The YCP and the Albanian Question, 114
Kosovë, 1945–1966, 116
Demands for an Albanian Republic, 120
Kosovë in the 1980s, 123
Conclusion, 130

Notes   133
Selected Bibliography   147
Index   151

Tables and Illustrations

Tables

1.1	Albanian vital population statistics	8
1.2	Age-specific statistics of Albania's population	8
1.3	Social composition of Albania's population, 1960–1985	9
2.1	Expansion of education in Albania	30
2.2	Women specialists with higher education	31
4.1	Membership of the APL, 1948–1986	56
4.2	APL Politburo and Secretariat, 1989	57
4.3	Composition of the Albanian government, 1989	60
5.1	Sources of national income	68
5.2	Specialists with higher education	69
5.3	Allocation of specialists with higher education	72

Maps

Albania	viii
Southeastern Europe	3

Photos

Enver Hoxha Museum, Tiranë	6
Castle in Shkodër	6
Gjirokastër	7
Shkodër	7

ALBANIA

International
boundary
National capital
Railroad
Road

YUGOSLAVIA

Bajram Curri

Koplik i Poshtém

Ishkodér

Puké

Kukés

Pruzen

Lezhé

Rréshen

Fush-Muhur

Dibra

YUGOSLAVIA

Laç

Burrel

Krujé

Vorë

TIRANÉ

Durrës

Librazhd

ADRIATIC

SEA

Rrogozhinë

Elbasan

Ohrid

LAKE
OHRID

Cérrik

Lin

Lushnje

Gramsh

Pogradec

Çëravë

LAKE
PRESPA

Fier

Stalin

Berat

Maliq

Korçë

Selinicë

Corovodë

Ersekë

Vlorë

Mavrovë

Këlcyrë

Përmet

Tepelenë

Laskovik

Himarë

Gjirokastër

GREECE

Jergucat

Kelpaki

Sarandë

CORFU

Ioannina

25 Miles

25 Kilometers

Source: U.S. Dept. of State Publication 8217, Background Notes Series

1

The Land and the People

The People's Socialist Republic of Albania (PSRA), the smallest and most isolated communist country, has attracted the attention of many foreign, particularly Western, observers with its maverick behavior within the international communist system and its rigid domestic policy. Between 1945 and 1985, under Enver Hoxha's leadership, Albania pursued a fiercely independent foreign policy. The PSRA has the unique distinction of having defied the three main centers of international communism: Yugoslavia, the Soviet Union, and China. Domestically, the ruling Albanian Party of Labor (APL) has faithfully implemented a strict Stalinist course and has carried out perhaps one of the most far-reaching social experiments in Eastern Europe.

Albania remained an enigma, one of the least known communist countries. Reliable information on internal developments was lacking and the selective and biased nature of the data released officially made it difficult to form a clear picture of the country. Before the mid-1980s, when Albania perceived itself in a state of international siege, few Western scholars and journalists were allowed to visit the PSRA. But with Hoxha's demise in April 1985 and Ramiz Alia's accession to power the situation appeared to be changing. By the end of the 1980s the Albanian mystery began to unravel as Alia's government embarked on a policy of general accommodation with other countries. Albania was no longer the hermit state it had been in the 1960s and the 1970s. Cultural, economic, and political interactions with the outside world increased and growing numbers of foreigners, particularly from Western Europe, visited the country. The internal atmosphere seemed perceptibly more relaxed than during Hoxha's era. If Albania remained the only Eastern European country that retained a rigidly centralized, Stalinist political system, it was obvious that the winds of change were beginning to blow new ideas into this orthodox communist state. While there was no suggestion the leadership would consider any weakening of communist rule, much less creation of a multiparty political system, Alia did advocate

1

new approaches in dealing with economic and political problems confronting the nation. Albania seemed determined, however, to move at
its own pace.

Alia inherited an array of seemingly inextricably intertwined problems. The rigid centralized economic system had led to a sluggish
economic performance, widening the gap between Albania and its
neighbors. The standard of living stagnated in the 1980s, mainly as a
result of the cessation of foreign assistance from China in 1978. Opportunities for social mobility also declined. After more than four decades
in power, the Communist regime was unable to meet the population's
basic material needs. Social malaise was pervasive, and significant
segments of the population, most notably the youth, seemed bent on
rejecting established regime values. But perhaps more important, the
social, political, and economic institutions, fashioned after the Stalinist
model, were not functioning well and were in dire need of change. The
outside world, particularly neighboring countries, continued to present
Albania with both challenges and opportunities.

The dramatic collapse in 1989 of communist rule in Poland, Hungary,
East Germany, Czechoslovakia, Bulgaria, and Romania caused deep
concern in Albania—Europe's last communist domino. The democratization in other Eastern European countries brought into question the
survival of the Albanian communist regime. Decades of totalitarian rule
had led Albania up a political and economic blind alley. Radical political
reform appeared to be anathema for the APL, which maintained that
its Marxist-Leninist ideology set it apart in a positive way from the
"revisionist" Communist parties in Eastern Europe and insisted its
socialist system had performed well. While Eastern Europe moved toward
democracy, Albania became an international pariah. Although the discontent generated by the contrasting freedoms and higher living standards
of other European countries had remained muted, the upheaval in Eastern
Europe had created a new reality for Albania. Tiranë's embattled leadership faced increasing internal demands and foreign pressure for change.
Only radical reforms will resolve the kinds of dilemmas that Albania
faced. The real question is whether the Albanian leadership can devise
policies that will somehow enable the APL to gain the confidence of
the population. Although in early 1990 there were no signs of organized
opposition and the secret police appeared all-pervasive, an opposition
movement could emerge very rapidly should dissidence arise as it did
in other East European states. It is doubtful that the Communist leadership
will be able to preserve the status quo for long and refuse to renounce
its exclusive hold on power without facing serious internal opposition.

The 1990s will represent a critical period for Albania. Alia will
have to make hard choices and chart a domestic and foreign policy

course that will lead the country into the next century. Albania's future will likely depend on whether Alia formulates and implements policies that will preserve the country's hard-won independence but, at the same time, will be more in line with current demands and requirements of Albanian society.

Western policymakers would be well advised to pay greater attention to Albania. Developments in that tiny country are likely to have implications beyond its borders. The United States and its allies in the North Atlantic Treaty Organization (NATO) have a high stake in the Balkans. Instability in Albania or the restoration of Soviet influence, coupled with the exacerbation of the ethnic conflict and economic crisis in Yugoslavia, could adversely affect the delicate balance of power in the volatile Balkans, long known as the "powder keg" of Europe.

GEOGRAPHICAL SETTING

Albania occupies a strategic position on the southern entrance to the Adriatic and is bounded to the north and east by Yugoslavia and to the south and east by Greece. The 1,204-km border with Yugoslavia runs northward from Lake Prespë to the Adriatic Sea, west of Shkodër. The border with Greece is 256 km long and runs southwest from Lake Prespë to the Ionian Sea. To the west and southwest, Albania is bordered by the Adriatic and Ionian seas. Its immediate western neighbor, Italy, lies less than 100 km away.

The smallest of the Balkan countries, Albania encompasses an area of 28,748 sq km, with a maximum length from north to south of about 340 km and a maximum width of about 150 km. It is predominantly a mountainous country with rugged terrain, which had hindered internal communication as well as the growth of national consciousness. The greater part of its territory, 76.6 percent, consists of mountains and hills over 200 meters above sea level; the remainder, 23.4 percent, consists of plains and valleys. The Alps of Albania, part of the Dinaric mountain system, extend over the northern portion of the country with elevations of close to 2,700 m. The region has limited arable land and is sparsely populated. Forestry and animal husbandry form the main economic activities. The central mountain region, extending from the valley of the

Drin River in the north to the central Devoll and the lower Osum valleys in the south, has a less rugged terrain and is more densely populated than the Alps region. It is characterized by substantial mineral deposits such as chromium, ferronickel, and copper. Forestry, animal husbandry, mining, and, to an extent, agriculture are the main economic resources of the region. South of the central mountain region there are a series of mountain ranges, with elevations of up to 2,500 m, and valleys. Although the Alps and the mountains of the central region are covered with dense forests, the mountains of the southern region are mostly bare and serve essentially as pasture for livestock. In contrast to the three mountain regions, western Albania, stretching along the Adriatic coast, consists of low-altitude, fertile plains. The most densely populated region in the country, this area extends over a distance of nearly 200 km from the western slopes of the North Alps south to the western slopes of the southern mountain region, penetrating to a depth of 50 km into the interior of the country. It is the most important agricultural and industrial area of the country. The 470-km-long Albanian littoral on the Adriatic is well known for its splendid beaches and the beauty of the surrounding landscape.

Endowed with considerable mineral resources, Albania can be divided into two distinct geological regions. The southwestern part of the country is rich in hydrocarbons and fuels, including oil and natural gas. The northeastern region has substantial reserves of chromite, copper, lignite, iron, and nickel. In the 1980s Albania was the world's third largest chromium producer.

The PSRA has a Mediterranean climate: Summers are generally hot and dry and winters mild, but with considerable variation from one region to another. The western part, under the influence of warm air masses from the sea, is the hottest, summer temperatures rising as high as 44°C and winter temperatures rarely falling below 0°C. The eastern part of the country is affected mainly by continental air masses and is characterized by cold winters, with temperatures falling as low as −26°C, and moderate summers, with temperatures generally below 35°C.

Rainfall in Albania is abundant but irregularly distributed throughout the year. Some 40 percent of the annual precipitation falls in the winter. Summer droughts are common, especially in the southwestern region. Albania is rich in rivers and streams; especially on the river Drin, the significant hydroelectric power potential has been exploited quite effectively, making the country an energy exporter. More than half of the arable land is irrigated with water from rivers and artificial reservoirs. Besides the Drin, other main rivers are the Seman, Shkumbin, and Vjosa. Albania also has many lakes, the most important of which are those of Shkodër, Pogradec, and Prespë.

The country is divided into twenty-six administrative districts, the largest and economically most important being those of Tiranë, Durrës, Shkodër, Elbasan, Vlorë, Korçë, and Fier. The capital, Tiranë, the country's main industrial and cultural center, in 1990 had a population of slightly more than 250,000. Other large cities include: Durrës (73,000), Shkodër (71,200), Elbasan (69,900), Vlorë (61,100), and Korçë (57,100).[1]

THE PEOPLE

In 1986 there were an estimated seven million Albanians in the world.[2] Ironically, more Albanians lived outside than within the boundaries of the Albanian state. Along almost all its borders with Yugoslavia were Albanian-speaking regions, which, in the opinion of most Albanians, should have been incorporated within the Albanian state when the Great Powers delimited its borders in 1913. According to the April 1989 census,[3] Albania had a population of 3,182,417, compared with 1,122,000 in 1945. Between 1979 and 1989, the population increased by 57,800 and was expected to reach four million by the year 2000. The PSRA had one of the most ethnically homogeneous populations in the world, with non-Albanians accounting for only 2 percent of the total population. In 1989 there were 58,758 ethnic Greeks, concentrated mainly in the Gjirokastër and Sarandë districts, and 4,797 Slavs, almost all of them Macedonians. The Albanian government actively encouraged population growth, and the population was increasing at an annual rate four to five times higher than the average in other European countries. Although during the 1970s and the early 1980s the annual population growth rate declined, in 1989 the birthrate was reported at 25.3 per thousand. According to statistics released by the Ministry of Health, mortality in 1988 was 5.4 per thousand. But despite improvements in health care, Albania had a high infant mortality rate: 25.3 per 1,000 live-born children. By 1989 life expectancy had reached seventy-two years (Table 1.1).[4] Albania had the youngest population in Europe: The average age of the population in 1985 was twenty-six years, with more than one third of the total population under fifteen years of age (Table 1.2). The majority of the population, 64.2 percent, lived in the countryside, and 35.5 percent in urban areas.[5] Workers accounted for 46.5 percent of the total population, peasants 42 percent, and the intelligentsia 11.5 percent (Table 1.3).

By 1990 the number of ethnic Albanians in Yugoslavia, inhabiting the province of Kosovë, western Macedonia, and southeastern and southwestern parts of Montenegro, had increased to more than 2.5 million, making them the country's third largest ethnic group. Although Albania and Kosovë had developed independently of each other since

Enver Hoxha Museum, Tiranë

Castle in Shkodër

Gjirokastër

Shkodër

TABLE 1.1
Albanian Vital Population Statistics
(per 1,000 of the population)

	1950	1960	1980	1989
Births	38.5	43.3	26.5	25.3
Deaths	14.0	10.4	6.4	5.4
Natural increase	24.5	32.9	20.1	20.0
Infant mortality	--	33.3	26.5	25.3
Life expectancy (in years)	53.5	64.9	69.5	72.0

Source: Vladimir Misja, Ylli Vejsiu, and Arqile Bërxholli, *Popullsia e Shqipërisë* [The Population of Albania] (Tiranë, 1987) pp. 22, 102, and 351; and *Zëri i Popullit*, June 21, 1989.

TABLE 1.2
Age-Specific Statistics of Albania's Population
(in percentages)

Age group	1965	1985
Under 15	42.2	33.9
15-29	24.3	29.8
30-44	15.7	17.4
45-59	10.1	11.3
Above 60	7.7	7.6

Source: Reproduced from Vladimir Misja, Ylli Vejsiu, and Arqile Bërxholli, *Popullsia e Shqipërisë* [The Population of Albania] (Tiranë, 1987), p. 169.

their forced partition in 1912, Albanians on both sides of the border viewed themselves as members of the same nation and used the same standard literary language. Demographic developments among the Albanians in Yugoslavia closely resembled those among their counterparts across the border. Population growth in Kosovë was slightly higher than in Albania: 29.9 per thousand (1987), making it among the highest in the world.[6] About 67 percent of the population lived in rural areas.[7] Sixty percent of Kosovë's total population was under twenty-seven years old. It is estimated that by the year 2000, the number of Albanians in Yugoslavia will reach four million.[8] Besides Albania and Kosovë, Italy, Greece, Turkey, and, to a lesser extent, Bulgaria and Romania also had

TABLE 1.3
Social Composition of Albania's Population, 1960-1985
(in percentages)

	1960	1969	1979	1985 (estimate)
Laborers	29.1	32.9	38.2	46.5
Peasants	41.6	55.4	50.2	42.0
White-collar workers	11.3	11.4	11.6	11.5
Other	18.0	--	--	--

Sources: Vladimir Misja, Ylli Vejsiu, and Arqile Bërxholli, Popullsia e Shqipërisë [The Population of Albania] (Tiranë, 1987), p. 216; and Harilla Papajorgji, Struktura socialklasore e klasës sonë punëtore [The Social and Class Composition of Our Working Class] (Tiranë: "8 Nëntori," 1985), p. 43.

large Albanian communities. There was also an ever-growing Albanian population in the United States.

The Albanians are divided into two subgroups, the Gegs and the Tosks, the Shkumbin River serving as a natural border between them. Differences in dialects used by the two groups as well as their different outlooks and ways of life were quite pronounced until the Communist regime sought to integrate the two groups and the terms Geg and Tosk disappeared from the political vocabulary. Before 1945, the more numerous Gegs, who inhabit northern Albania, Kosovë, western parts of Macedonia, and southern parts of Montenegro, traditionally dominated Albanian politics. Well known for their independent spirit and fighting abilities, the Gegs managed to enjoy a great degree of independence and opposed the authority of foreign invaders and, subsequently, that of the Albanian government. Before the Communist takeover, the Geg society was organized according to tribal groups, with the clan chieftain, bajraktar, playing an important political and social role. While the clan system and the traditional Geg way of life had largely disappeared in Albania by the end of the 1980s, the patriarchal family system was still evident among ethnic Albanians in Yugoslavia.

The Tosks live in southern Albania and parts of northern Greece. Because their territories were easily accessible, the Tosks had substantial contacts with the outside world and, as a result, foreign influences among them were more pronounced than among the Gegs. During the interwar period, the south was characterized by a semifeudal society. The peasantry, which made up the majority of the population, was exploited by a small group of large landowners, who controlled about two-thirds of the rich land. The communist movement was largely based in the south, and, before Enver Hoxha's death, most influential party and government posts were generally held by Tosks.

Albania is Europe's only predominantly Moslem country—a legacy of nearly five centuries of Ottoman rule. At the end of World War II, some 70 percent of the population was Moslem, 20 percent Albanian Orthodox, and 10 percent Roman Catholic. The Catholics inhabit the northern districts of the country and, across the border, Montenegro and Kosovë; members of the Orthodox church live in the southern districts of Gjirokastër, Korçë, Berat, and Vlorë. The Albanians had traditionally displayed a high degree of religious tolerance, and religious diversity did not obstruct national unity. The motto of the founding fathers of modern Albania was "The religion of the Albanians is Albanianism." For the Albanians the main identification was to be ethnonational rather than religious. Nevertheless, soon after it seized power, the Communist regime launched a campaign against religious institutions. In 1967 Albania became the world's first self-proclaimed atheist country. All religious institutions were closed, church property confiscated, and religious practices prohibited. Hoxha's policy of supplanting religion with communist ideology failed, however, and by the end of the 1980s officials acknowledged that Albania was experiencing a religious revival. Under Ramiz Alia's rule, the antireligious campaign continued but was significantly less intensive than during his predecessor's era. In August 1989 the government permitted Mother Teresa, the Albanian-born nun and winner of the Nobel Peace Prize, to visit Tiranë. Although the visit was termed private, Mother Teresa was received by the Albanian foreign minister and Nexhmije Hoxha, the widow of the former leader. With freedom of religion denied in Albania, Albanian émigrés abroad kept their religious beliefs alive. In the United States alone, dozens of churches and mosques were built by Albanian communities.

The Communist regime devoted considerable attention to the cultural and educational development of the country. In 1945 about 80 percent of the population was illiterate; by the end of the 1980s the authorities claimed illiteracy had practically been eliminated.

EARLY HISTORY

Most scholars are of the opinion that the Albanians are descendants of the Illyrians, an Indo-European people who settled the western part of the Balkan Peninsula at, or shortly after, the end of the Bronze Age (about 1000 B.C.). Albanians themselves, both in the PSRA and in Kosovë, invested considerable resources in archeological research to corroborate the thesis of Albania's ancient civilization and document the continuity between the Illyrians and the Albanians. The Albanians refer to themselves as *shqiptarë* and to their country as *Shqipëri*. *Albania*, the term used by foreigners to refer to the country, derived from *Albanoi*, the name of an Illyrian tribe, which was said to have inhabited present-day central Albania.

The Illyrians established their own states during the fifth and the third centuries B.C. The Adrians kingdom, founded in the third century B.C., was the most prominent. It extended from the Dalmatian coast to the coastal regions of present-day Albania and reached the peak of its power during King Agron's reign (250–231 B.C.). The Adrians kingdom was a major naval power, preying on Roman ships and thus endangering the Roman republic's trade. In 168 B.C. Rome conquered the entire Illyrian kingdom and thereafter ruled it for more than five centuries. In the beginning of the Roman occupation, Albania became an important center, connecting Rome with Byzantium by its Via Egnatia. The Illyrians played a significant role in the Roman Empire. Several of the emperors were of Illyrian origin, the most prominent of them Claudius II, Aurelian, Diocletian, and Probus in the third century A.D., Constantine the Great in the fourth century, and Justinian in the sixth century.

With the division of the Roman Empire in A.D. 395, Albania was made part of the Eastern Empire. Albanian ports became important trade centers, and during this period Durrës (Durrachium) and some other cities reached the heights of their prosperity. As the Roman Empire declined, the Illyrian provinces were invaded by migrating tribes vying for control of the western parts of the Balkans. The Goths and Huns came in the fourth century, and the Bulgars in the fifth century. During the sixth and seventh centuries large numbers of Slavs began to penetrate Illyrian territories. Faced with the danger of assimilation, the Albanians, who had by this time converted to Christianity, moved southward, concentrating mainly in the rugged mountain regions, where they remained nominally under the rule of the East Roman, or Byzantine, Empire.

During the eleventh and twelfth centuries Albania was overrun by the Normans. But in 1190, during a period of Byzantine weakness, the Albanian prince Progon established an independent state. This lasted until the middle of the thirteenth century, after which the country relapsed into disunity. In the fourteenth century Albania was conquered by the Serbs. With the collapse of Stephan Dushan's Serbian Empire in 1355, Albania fell under the domination of local feudal lords. The Topias and the Dukagjinis ruled in the north, the Muzakas and the Shpatas in the south.

The Ottoman Turks invaded Albania at the end of the fourteenth century. Under the leadership of Gjergj Kastrioti Skënderbeu (Scanderbeg), the Albanians waged a successful twenty-five-year struggle against Turkish occupation. In 1448 and in 1466 Skënderbeu repulsed large Turkish expeditions, but after his death in 1468, Albania became part of the Ottoman Empire. A large number of Albanians immigrated to Italy, and the majority of the population converted to Islam. During the nearly five centuries of Turkish occupation, many Albanians rose to high positions in the empire. Nevertheless, given Albania's rugged topography and its people's determination to preserve their autonomy, the Turks were never able to establish total control over the country. During the later part of the eighteenth century, several native princes rose to prominence. From 1775 to 1796, the Bushatis ruled the Shkodër duchy, extending their authority over northern and central Albania. From 1790 to 1822, Ali Pasha ruled the duchy of Janina, which extended from Vlorë and Berat to Çamëria and Thessaly.

NATIONAL AWAKENING AND INDEPENDENCE

The first signs of an organized Albanian nationalist movement appeared in the late 1800s. In June 1878 representatives from all over Albania met at Prizren, Kosovë, and established the Albanian League, also known as the Prizren League. With branches all over Albania, the league's primary objectives were to prevent the cession of Albanian-inhabited regions to Montenegro and Serbia and obtain administrative autonomy from Turkey. Although it succeeded in frustrating most, but by no means all, Great Power plans to hand over Albanian territories to its neighbors, the league failed in its attempts to gain administrative and cultural autonomy from Turkey and to unite Albanian lands into one *vilajet* (province). The Turks crushed the league in 1881 and imprisoned or killed its leaders, yet the movement had a lasting impact and would inspire later nationalist activity, especially in the northwest and northeast regions, such as Kosovë, which continued to face the threat of occupation by Serbia and Montenegro.

On November 28, 1912, after a series of revolts originating in Kosovë and after the Balkan states had declared war on Turkey, Albanian patriots led by Ismail Qemal proclaimed the country's independence. Their dream of incorporating all predominantly Albanian-inhabited territories into one state were shattered, however, as Serbia, Montenegro, and Greece occupied large parts of Albania. At the London Conference in December 1912, the Great Powers recognized Albania's independence. But the 1913 frontier demarcation by a special commission appointed by the Great Powers excluded from Albania more than half of its territory, including Kosovë and Çamëria (in the south) and about 40 percent of its people.

The Great Powers selected the German prince Wilhelm zu Wied as Albania's ruler. He arrived in Durrës in March 1914 but, because of local opposition and the outbreak of World War I, fled the country six months later. During the war, Albania became a battlefield for the belligerent powers. With the coming of peace, it again faced the prospect of dismemberment by its neighbors. The Paris Peace Conference, however, rejected claims put forth by Greece, Serbia and Montenegro, and Italy, and Albania was saved from further partition.

At the Congress of Lushnje, in January 1920, the Albanians established a provisional government and a council of regency; the following summer Italy recognized Albania's independence. During the next four years Albania was beset by a fierce struggle for power among competing political factions. By 1925 Ahmet Zogu had achieved preeminence. He ruled the country first as president, but from 1928 to 1939 as Zog I, King of the Albanians, a title that symbolically embraced the Albanian minorities in Yugoslavia and Greece. King Zog inherited a semifeudal society with widespread poverty, high illiteracy, and a backward economy. He imposed law and order, introduced a series of cultural and economic reforms, and laid the foundations of a modern state. His rule was characterized by what Stavro Skendi described as "a strange combination of Oriental rule and Western reform. The methods of government were those inherited from the corrupt Ottoman Empire."[9] King Zog transformed the parliament into a rubber-stamp body, exercised absolute power, and dealt ruthlessly with his political adversaries. Attempts to introduce political reforms or democratize the society were thwarted by remnants of the old aristocracy and conservative forces. In the realm of foreign policy, King Zog's options were limited as the Great Powers and the League of Nations refused to provide badly needed economic assistance. He entered into a political and military alliance with fascist Italy. Heavy economic dependence on Rome in turn led to Italian interference in Albania's domestic and foreign affairs and, in April 1939, to its annexation.

Albania's turbulent historical experience—the loss of Kosovë and other predominantly Albanian-inhabited territories, persistent threats to its independence, and the prospect of further dismemberment—augmented a defensive nationalism among the Albanians, strengthening in the face of enormous odds their determination to reestablish and sustain their country's independence. Perhaps more than any other factor, nationalism, fueled by a sense of justified grievances, would influence Albania's future Communist leaders as they charted a new course for their country.

2

Albania Under Hoxha

Enver Hoxha, the founder and lifelong leader of the Albanian Communist Party (ACP), ruled Albania longer than any other person in its entire history: from November 1944 until his death in April 1985. More than any other member of the ruling elite, Hoxha was responsible for charting Albania's post–World War II course, which he considered to be the world's only genuine Marxist-Leninist path. He imposed on his country one of the most rigorous forms of communism the world had seen. After a series of dramatic alignments and dealignments with other communist countries, Hoxha isolated his country from the mainstream of international politics, reducing Albania's external interactions to the bare minimum.

Under his leadership, the ruling ACP instituted a highly centralized polity in which the party sought to control all aspects of life, leaving little room for social and individual initiatives. Crafty and ruthless, Hoxha employed terror and coercion to impose a totalitarian system that denied his people the most basic rights. At the same time, Albania made significant headway in the economic and educational spheres. Moreover, through his maneuvers and wholesale alterations of the pattern of Tiranë's external relations, Hoxha succeeded in making Albania a truly independent country—no mean achievement for a small state whose modern history was replete with examples of domination, perpetual insults, and repeated attempts at dismemberment by its more powerful neighbors. But despite undisputable progress, Hoxha left his successors a legacy of repression; party factionalism; multiple economic, social, and political problems; technological backwardness; and isolation from and fear of the outside world.

Upon his accession to power, Ramiz Alia described Hoxha as "the greatest son" Albania had ever given birth to.[1] Kosovar scholar and diplomat Ramadan Marmullaku considered Hoxha "the only Albanian of world stature," a leader who in many respects exemplified "the spirit of his people," "an intellectual par excellence," and a "skillful politician and pragmatist."[2] Peter R. Prifti, a long-time observer of Albanian affairs, characterized him as "a skillful organizer and versatile politician" and "a nationalist [and] a doctrinaire communist" who strongly believed "in the efficacy of radical measures for the modernization of Albania."[3] Hoxha's political adversaries depicted him as an incomparable dictator in Albania's history.[4] Other observers have noted Hoxha's complex and contradictory personality.[5] But whatever opinion one holds of Hoxha and the policies and methods he applied to achieve his objectives, one cannot understand developments in socialist Albania without a review of how he came to power and the unique path he laid for his country.

THE ROAD TO POWER

Most of the information regarding Hoxha's childhood and early revolutionary activity comes from his own memoirs, which were periodically updated and republished to fit subsequent developments. Sulo Gradeci, who served for three decades as Hoxha's personal guard, has provided some interesting insights regarding Hoxha's personality, work habits, relations with family members and coworkers, and health problems. According to Gradeci, Hoxha was an ardent reader and a hard worker. Taken as a whole, however, Gradeci's book is predictably slanted in favor of Hoxha and attributes all of Albania's "achievements" to the late dictator and all its "failures" to his opponents.[6]

Son of a farmer, Enver Hoxha was born on October 16, 1908, in the southern city of Gjirokastër, a center of Albanian nationalism. His family was relatively affluent. His father had emigrated to the United States, where he had worked for a time and then returned to Albania. The individual who exerted the greatest influence on Hoxha during his childhood was, according to his memoirs, his uncle Hysen Hoxha, an atheist but a devoted Albanian patriot. Through his uncle he was imbued with a strong sentiment of Albanian nationalism and the determination to fight foreigners bent on dominating and partitioning Albania.[7]

After his secondary education in Albania, Hoxha received a scholarship from King Zog's government to study abroad. He studied in France for several years but never earned a degree. His procommunist leanings can be traced to this period of his life that included a short tour of duty in the Albanian legation in Brussels.[8] Under a pseudonym, he reportedly wrote articles on Albania for the French Communist Party newspaper, L'Humanité.[9] These articles were never republished in Albania, although some eighty volumes of Hoxha's collected works, including memoirs, diaries, speeches, conversations, and articles, appeared between 1968 and 1989. Upon his return to Albania in 1936, Hoxha briefly taught French in Tiranë and then in Korçë.

At the time Hoxha went to study in France, the general situation in Albania was unfavorable. The standard of living was considerably lower than that of the neighboring countries, and most of the population lived at the subsistence level. Moreover, the country had become dangerously dependent politically and economically on fascist Italy. The conditions he found in France evidently had a great impact on Hoxha: From a semifeudal society he suddenly found himself in a modern industrialized society with a relative abundance of material goods. This cultural shock, coupled with his strong nationalistic sentiments, probably more than anything else convinced Hoxha of the need to search for a shortcut approach in getting Albania out of what he considered a hopeless situation. With his leftist political inclinations, Hoxha took Joseph Stalin's forced industrialization to be the best model. Long after the Soviet dictator had been condemned in his own country for the serious transgressions and the vicious crimes he had perpetrated, Hoxha remained an implacable Stalinist.

Albania had not been a suitable ground for the spread of Marxist ideas because of its economic and political underdevelopment. Predominantly an agrarian society, with high illiteracy and only a minor industrial base, Albania lacked a developed proletariat. Nevertheless, by the end of the 1930s, several communist groups had emerged.[10] These groups exercised no significant influence among the masses, were in constant disagreement among themselves, and initially made no effort to resist the Italian invasion of Albania in April 1939.

Beginning in September 1939, Albanian communist groups established a liaison, through Kosovar communists, with the Yugoslav Communist Party (YCP), which had been directed by the Comintern to assist in the formation of an Albanian party.[11] After long negotiations and direct assistance from Yugoslav Communist envoys Dušan Mugoša and Miladin Popović,[12] representatives of the most important communist groups met on November 8, 1941, and formed the ACP. Significantly, the majority of these Communists were intellectuals, which subsequently would make the initially more orthodox Yugoslav and Soviet Communist leaders suspicious of them, particularly Hoxha. None of the seven members of the Provisional Central Committee had been to the Soviet Union. In this respect, the ACP held the unique distinction of being the only Communist party in Europe where the Soviets had played no direct role in its formation.

At the time of the founding of the ACP, Hoxha was not Albania's most renowned Communist. But because the most prominent Communists were deeply involved in the polemics and feuds of the different communist groups, Hoxha emerged as the only acceptable compromise candidate for the top party post. At the first party conference in March 1943,

Hoxha was formally named general secretary, a position he held until his demise. From its inception, however, the party was plagued with factional struggles. Hoxha's leadership continued to be challenged throughout the war period, with the Yugoslavs playing a major behind-the-scenes role in attempts to undermine his position.

Under Communist auspices, the National Liberation Front (NLF) was formed in September 1942, the ACP declaring that they had reached an agreement with other patriotic forces fighting the occupiers. The Communists launched their resistance movement against the invaders with the creation of the National Liberation Army in July 1943. The Allied command in Italy supplied considerable material assistance during the war; significantly, Albanian Communists received no support, military or otherwise, from the Soviet Union. In September 1943, preparing the ground for a seizure of power following the anticipated defeat of Germany, the Communists launched a campaign against the nationalist organization Balli Kombëtar (National Front) and the pro–King Zog Legaliteti (Legality) movement. After a bloody civil war, both groups were defeated, and by October 1944 the Communists were able to form a provisional government headed by Hoxha. A month later, they took control of the entire country.

The ACP emerged from the war under strong Yugoslav influence. Through its emissaries Mugoša and Popović, who stayed in Albania until late 1944, the YCP had played a prominent role in ACP's affairs, exerting considerable influence on its decisionmaking process. The Yugoslavs mistrusted Hoxha because of his intellectual and bourgeois background and attempted to replace him with Politburo member and party organizational secretary Koçi Xoxe, who was more pliable to their objectives. Hoxha garnered the Yugoslavs' wrath in particular because of his stand toward the nationalists: He apparently favored accommodation, whereas the Yugoslavs fiercely objected to any power-sharing arrangements between Albanian communists and nationalists because the latter insisted that Kosovë, which in 1941 had been incorporated into Albania, remain part of Albania after the war. In 1943 the ACP reached an agreement with the Balli Kombëtar, which provided for the establishment of a Committee of National Salvation and called for a plebiscite to decide whether the Kosovars wanted to remain under Yugoslav rule or unite with their mother country, Albania, after the war. The Yugoslavs were also concerned that if Albanian Communists shared power with Balli Kombëtar in the Committee of National Salvation, the prospects for Communist takeover in Albania would be undermined. Recognizing the anti-Yugoslav sentiments among ethnic Albanians, Yugoslav Communists, having by this time decided on the establishment of a federal state, apparently feared that, given a choice, the Kosovars would opt for union with Albania. Under pressure from the Yugoslavs, Hoxha was forced to denounce the agreement with the Balli Kombëtar. The Yugoslavs sidetracked the Kosovë question, insisting the issue would be solved after the war. By November 1944 the Yugoslavs had succeeded in creating a pro-Yugoslav faction, headed by Xoxe, within the Albanian party Politburo, and Hoxha's position was seriously undermined.

POLITICAL DEVELOPMENTS, 1945–1960

With the installation of the Communist government, the ACP took immediate measures to consolidate its power. Remnants of the nationalist parties and the prewar political elite were eliminated through military action, show trials, and a campaign of terror and intimidation. What was deemed excessive wealth in private property was confiscated without compensation, all industrial plants and mines were nationalized, and a radical agrarian reform was instituted. On January 11, 1946, a constituent assembly, elected the previous month, proclaimed Albania a people's republic. In March a new constitution, modeled closely after that of Yugoslavia, was promulgated and a new government formed, with Hoxha as prime minister and his rival, Xoxe, in charge of the Ministry of Internal Affairs and thus in control of the widely feared secret police, the Sigurimi.

The new regime was faced with grave domestic and foreign policy problems. In many parts of the country, the government met with armed opposition, and the economy was in shambles. Athens, which considered itself in a state of war with Tiranë because the Italians had staged their invasion of Greece from occupied Albania, renewed its territorial claims to southern Albania. Tiranë's relations with the United States were complicated by Albania's refusal to accept the validity of pre–World War II bilateral treaties and agreements. And ties with Britain were strained after a British ship hit a mine off Albania's coast, killing forty-four sailors.

The regime's quandary was further compounded by policy disputes within the top leadership and the emergence of two distinct factions in the Politburo. One faction, whose most articulate advocate was Sejfulla Malëshova, insisted that Albania pursue an independent foreign policy, developing close relations with both the East and the West, and follow a moderate domestic policy. The more powerful and pro-Yugoslav faction, headed by Xoxe, advocated a close alliance with Belgrade and the implementation of radical social and economic policies similar to those being carried out by the Yugoslav regime. In February 1946 Malëshova was expelled from the Politburo and the party on charges of "rightist opportunism."[13] Hoxha, who initially was more closely identified with the moderates, came under pressure from the Yugoslavs. Josip Djerdja, the Yugoslav envoy in Tiranë, said in June 1946 that "instead of a resolute and undoubting orientation toward the East, toward Yugoslavia, the democratic Balkans, and the USSR . . . some Albanian statesmen turned their eyes more toward the West." He accused the Albanian leaders of plunging themselves "into a political play without principles and a speculation with the West following the slogan 'all for the international recognition of our independence!'"[14]

Following Malëshova's purge, Albania's relations with Western powers deteriorated dramatically. U.S. and British representatives were accused of having instigated a series of small-scale uprisings in Albania, and Western powers rejected Albania's application for membership in the United Nations. Both the United States and Great Britain withdrew their representatives from Tiranë.

It was against this background that in July 1946 Albania and Yugoslavia signed a Treaty of Friendship, Cooperation, and Mutual Aid. This was followed by the signing of a series of treaties closely binding the political, military, and economic systems of the two countries. Albania became so dependent on Belgrade that the Yugoslavs exercised preponderant influence over many sectors of the Albanian society—much more so than did the Italians in the prewar period. Yugoslav domination extended to the political, economic, military, and cultural spheres. Serbo-Croat was introduced as a required subject in Albanian high schools, many Albanians were sent to Yugoslavia for training and education, and Yugoslav experts were brought in to help Albania. From 1945 until 1948, Albania lost many of the characteristics of a sovereign state. By spring 1948 plans were underway for Albania's "union" with Yugoslavia. According to Milovan Djilas, then a senior member of the Yugoslav leadership, Belgrade advocated the idea because such an arrangement

> would not only be of direct value to both Yugoslavia and Albania, but would also finally put an end to the traditional intolerance and conflict between Serbs and Albanians. Its particular importance . . . lay in the fact that it would make possible the amalgamation of [Yugoslavia's] considerable and compact Albanian minority with Albania as a separate republic in the Yugoslav-Albanian Federation. Any other solution to the problem of the Albanian national minority seemed impracticable . . . since the simple transfer of Yugoslav territories inhabited by Albanians would give rise to uncontrollable resistance in the Yugoslav Communist Party itself.[15]

Yugoslavia's tenacious efforts to force the Albanian government to accept a merger of the two countries caused widespread opposition both within the ACP leadership and among the populace. The long-term effect of this misguided policy was to exacerbate the deep-rooted animosity between Albanians and Slavs, entangling Tiranë-Belgrade relations for decades to come. Hoxha recognized the dangers that Yugoslav aims represented for him personally and for his country's independence. But during the most critical periods of Yugoslav pressure he never took a clear-cut, public stand against Yugoslav aggrandizement, as did some members of the leadership, including Nako Spiru, who, isolated and faced with the prospect of being purged and perhaps put on trial, committed suicide. Instead, Hoxha worked behind the scenes, seeking to enlist Soviet support. With Yugoslavia's expulsion from the Cominform, Hoxha lost no time in denouncing his former benefactors, making Albania the first Eastern European country to publicly condemn Belgrade. The Albanian government expelled all Yugoslav advisers and experts, and unilaterally denounced all economic treaties, agreements, and protocols concluded with Yugoslavia, with the exception of the 1946 treaty of friendship, which was renounced by Belgrade in November 1949.

Hoxha moved swiftly to consolidate his position within the party and the government. Xoxe and his closest associates were dismissed from their posts and replaced with Hoxha loyalists. Xoxe was tried and later executed. At Stalin's suggestion, the Communist party was renamed the Albanian Party of Labor at its first congress, held in November 1948.

The break with Yugoslavia signified the elevation of Albania from a Yugoslav subsatellite to a Soviet satellite. Albania came to play an important role in Stalin's strategy of isolating and coercing Yugoslavia. Tiranë received substantial economic and military assistance from the Soviet Union and its allies and embarked upon an ambitious industrialization program with the objective of transforming Albania from an underdeveloped agrarian country to an agricultural-industrial state. It institutionalized, with minor modifications, the Soviet system of centralized economic planning, emphasizing the rapid development of heavy industry at the expense of agricultural development. In 1949 Albania joined the Council of Mutual Economic Assistance (CMEA).

A founding member of the Warsaw Pact Treaty Organization, Albania enjoyed cordial relations with the Soviet Union between 1948 and 1955. It faithfully supported both Soviet foreign and domestic policies. Soviet influence in Albania's domestic affairs, exerted through the many economic, technical, and military experts and advisers, was quite pervasive. But with Stalin's death and the advent of a more pragmatic leadership in Moscow (interested in rapprochement with Yugoslavia), Albania ceased to play a significant role in the Soviet Union's Balkan strategy. Hoxha and his supporters were distressed by the 1955 visit to Belgrade of

Soviet leader Nikita S. Khrushchev, which was followed almost immediately by Moscow's calls for a normalization of Albanian-Yugoslav ties and pressures for the rehabilitation of Xoxe and other victims of the post-1948 purges. Other members of the Albanian leadership, however, encouraged by Moscow's new policy toward Belgrade and a more relaxed internal policy, called for a reassessment of Tiranë's post-1948 policy. Politburo members Bedri Spahiu and Tuk Jakova favored rapprochement with Yugoslavia and urged that the government pursue a more moderate socioeconomic policy. Hoxha succeeded in rallying enough support at a meeting of the Central Committee in April 1955 to dislodge both Spahiu and Jakova.[16] Still, he not only failed to come out openly against the Soviet-Yugoslav rapprochement but resorted to a tactic that had served him well in past difficult circumstances: He prudently admitted that mistakes had been made, blaming "imperialist agents" for the 1948 break between Yugoslavia and the rest of the bloc.[17] But although Tiranë-Belgrade polemics subsided, there was no appreciable improvement in their relations.

Hoxha experienced increased external and domestic pressures for a policy reassessment, particularly following Khrushchev's secret speech at the Twentieth Congress of the Soviet Communist Party in which he denounced Stalin. He faced the most serious challenge to his position at a conference of the Tiranë party organization in April 1956. Echoing developments in the Soviet Union, Hoxha's opponents criticized his leadership style and insisted that the APL policy be analyzed in light of the de-Stalinization campaign in the Soviet Union. This serious internal challenge to Hoxha coincided with Khrushchev's persistent pressures, probably at Belgrade's insistence, to rehabilitate Xoxe. Thanks to Moscow's more relaxed grip on the Eastern European states and his shrewd political maneuvering, Hoxha successfully withstood both these challenges. He dealt swiftly and ruthlessly with his opponents, who lacked effective leadership and organization.[18]

Developments in Hungary and Poland in 1956 only served to reinforce Hoxha's opposition to Khrushchev's foreign and domestic policies. Both the Soviet-Yugoslav rapprochement and Khrushchev's de-Stalinization campaign threatened Hoxha's tenure in office and perhaps even his life. With fresh memories of Yugoslav domination before 1948, Hoxha apparently feared that Khrushchev and Tito might reach an understanding giving the latter a free hand in Albania. An implementation of a de-Stalinization campaign in Albania, where Hoxha and his closest collaborators, Mehmet Shehu, Hysni Kapo, and Beqir Balluku, had developed an extensive personality cult and instituted a reign of terror, threatened the very foundations of the regime. In defending Stalin, therefore, Hoxha was defending his regime's blemished record. He was determined to ensure that developments in Hungary and Poland were not repeated in Albania.

He immediately launched a public campaign against Yugoslavia, blaming Tito's "revisionist" ideas for the ferment in Eastern Europe. At the same time, he began to turn to the Chinese in an effort to enlist their support against Soviet pressures. Although for a time it appeared that Khrushchev and Hoxha had reached an accommodation and the Soviets and their allies increased significantly their assistance to Albania, Tiranë's defiance of Moscow became more pronounced. In addition to disagreements over de-Stalinization and Yugoslavia, Tiranë and Moscow took divergent stands on other important issues. The Albanians criticized Khrushchev's adoption of peaceful coexistence with the capitalist world as the general foreign policy line of the Soviet bloc. They also rejected Khrushchev's proposition, elaborated at the Twentieth Congress of the Soviet Communist Party, that the possibility existed for a peaceful transition to socialism. On all these issues, the APL leadership took an extreme leftist position. If such a position brought Tiranë into direct conflict with Moscow, it pointed to a commonality of interest with the Chinese.

Disenchanted with Tiranë's domestic and foreign policies, the Soviets resorted to punitive political and economic measures, causing Albania serious economic problems. When it became obvious in 1960 that Hoxha was going to persevere in his defiance of the Soviet Union, Moscow attempted to encourage members of the leadership to unite and overthrow Hoxha. Moreover, the Soviets apparently used their influence within the Albanian armed forces to agitate against Hoxha. Soviet attempts failed, however, because Hoxha, cognizant of the upcoming rift with the Soviets, had taken measures to strengthen his stranglehold on the leadership, having purged pro-Soviet elements within the top echelons of the party and the government.

It was during 1960 that Albania took a clear-cut stand in favor of China in the intensified Sino-Soviet conflict. Relations between the two giant Communist states had been burdened by China's disillusionment with Khrushchev's leadership of the international Communist movement, policy differences regarding the United States and the Third World, Soviet failure to provide the Chinese with adequate economic assistance, and the long-standing border dispute. As Albanian sympathy drifted toward the Chinese, the Soviets responded by suspending their economic and military assistance, withdrawing all experts, and effectively barring Albania from the Warsaw Pact and CMEA. Finally, in December 1961, in an unprecedented development between socialist states, the Soviet Union broke diplomatic relations with Albania. Moscow's Eastern European allies recalled their ambassadors from Tiranë but stopped short of a total break in diplomatic and economic relations. All contacts between Albania and Eastern Europe, however, were sharply reduced.

ALBANIA'S ROAD TO SELF-ASSERTION

Tiny Albania paid a heavy price in political, economic, and military terms for its defiance of the USSR. Nevertheless, it emerged from this dispute with a greater degree of independence than ever before in its history. The Albanian propaganda machine portrayed the break with the Soviet Union as one of the most significant events in the nation's history, acclaiming Hoxha as the "savior" of the country's independence.

The Chinese moved quickly to fill in the gap left by the withdrawal of Soviet and Eastern European experts.[19] Despite serious domestic difficulties, throughout the 1960s the Chinese granted Albania substantial economic and military aid on generous terms, in the form of either interest-free or low-interest credits and grants. The two countries shared a basic consensus on major domestic and foreign policy issues, the most significant bond being their common alienation from Moscow. Albania, for its part, adhered closely to Beijing's international position and served as China's representative at the United Nations and other international organizations from which the People's Republic of China (PRC) was barred. High-level party and government delegations were exchanged quite frequently, especially during China's Cultural Revolution.

In the initial stages of the alliance there were some notable differences in the two countries' stands, conditioned by their different national interests and perceptions. Until the mid-1960s, the Chinese, unlike their Albanian allies, were reluctant to initiate a full break with the Soviets and attempted to reach an accommodation with the Kremlin. With the resumption of public Sino-Soviet polemics in late 1964 and the shattering of hopes for a Beijing-Moscow rapprochement in the wake of Khrushchev's ouster, a close convergence developed in Albanian and Chinese positions regarding many foreign and domestic policy issues. The two allies launched a fierce ideological campaign against Soviet "revisionism," accusing the Soviet leadership of having betrayed Marxism-Leninism and opened the doors for the restoration of capitalism in the USSR and the Eastern European countries. They challenged Moscow's influence in the international Communist movement by inciting opposition groups and factions within many pro-Soviet Communist parties and encouraging the formation of what they termed "genuine," splinter, Marxist-Leninist parties. The two allies also waged a propaganda war against the United States. Albania's enmity toward the United States stemmed from the cold war and was reinforced by continued U.S. support for Yugoslavia. China, on the other hand, considered the United States its principal enemy because of U.S. support for Taiwan and its strategy in Vietnam. Subscribing to what they called the "dual-adversary" theory, Tiranë and Beijing considered the struggles against the two superpowers as inseparable.

Chinese assistance proved indispensable for Albania's economic development. The Albanians, however, were forced to scale down their ambitious industrial development goals. The aid Albania received from China was of considerably lower quality than that received from the Soviets. In addition, China's poor coordination of the construction of industrial projects and the belated arrival of Chinese supplies caused delays in the completion of various projects, readjustments in investments and construction, and contributed to Albania's failure to achieve major objectives.

By the mid-1960s Hoxha's regime was faced with popular dissatisfaction and major domestic difficulties. Economic performance was disappointing, and the leadership's power was apparently being undermined. In order to reassert his authority, Hoxha launched a "Cultural and Ideological Revolution" whose objectives were to prevent the emergence of revisionism and the restoration of capitalism in Albania, eliminate potential alternative power centers that might conceivably threaten APL control over all aspects of the society, and forestall the emergence of a "new class" by streamlining the bureaucracy. No sector of the society was left untouched. The military was especially hard hit: All military ranks were abolished, party committees were established in army units, and political commissars were introduced into military headquarters at all levels. The military's role in the Albanian polity was decreased, and professionalism in the military establishment was relegated to a position secondary to ideology and economics. The leadership also launched an antireligious campaign, which resulted in the 1967 proclamation of Albania as the world's only atheistic state; proceeded to fully collectivize agriculture; initiated a campaign for the emancipation of women; and carried out a reform of the educational system to rid it of Soviet influence.

Although at the time it was widely believed that Albania's Cultural Revolution was inspired by China's Cultural Revolution, there were significant differences between the two movements. Hoxha, unlike Mao, maintained tight control over the implementation of the Cultural Revolution. In contrast to developments in the PRC, Albania's revolution did not affect its foreign policy nor did it lead to a domestic political convulsion and the weakening of party influence.[20]

The Soviet-led, Warsaw Pact invasion of Czechoslovakia in 1968 had a great and lasting impact on the Albanian-Chinese alliance. In the short term the invasion brought the two countries closer together. China hailed Albania's formal withdrawal from the Warsaw Pact, promised to come to its assistance in the event of a Soviet invasion, and took measures to strengthen Albania's defense capabilities. The long-term impact of the invasion of Czechoslovakia, however, was to force both Beijing and Tiranë to reevaluate their relationship in particular and their foreign policy posture in general. Once the crisis subsided, China sought to decrease its military commitment to Albania and to improve relations with Yugoslavia and Romania in an attempt to undermine the Soviet Union's position in the Balkans.

Perceptions of an increased Soviet military threat made the Albanians realize that reliance for protection on distant and militarily weak China was an insufficient guarantee of Albania's security. Thus, they began to seek an accommodation with their neighbors and with selected Western European and Third World countries. By 1971 Tiranë had normalized relations with Yugoslavia and Greece. China welcomed Albania's cautious opening up to the outside world. For its part, Albania was less enthusiastic about China's rapid improvement of relations with Yugoslavia and its proposal that Albania seek a military alliance with Yugoslavia and Romania against a potential Soviet attack. Despite Tiranë's reconciliation with Belgrade and pledge to come to its assistance in the event of a Soviet invasion, Albania was not interested in an alliance with its more powerful neighbor, with which it had important political and ideological differences.

In the beginning of the 1970s, the Chinese initiated radical changes in their foreign policy, abandoning their isolationist stance and taking measures to return to the mainstream of international politics. Albanian-Chinese relations were profoundly affected by U.S. President Richard M. Nixon's visit to Beijing in 1972. In its rapprochement with the United States, China took a unilateral action without consulting or informing Albania in advance, causing Hoxha to draw an analogy with the 1955 Soviet-Yugoslav rapprochement. While sharing Beijing's concern about the Soviet threat, Tiranë did not believe there was a significant decrease in the U.S. threat to warrant—as Chinese policy pronouncements then reflected—the transformation of Washington from a primary adversary to a lesser one. Hoxha maintained the two superpowers were equally dangerous and refused to differentiate between their "imperialist" policies. At the Sixth APL Congress in November 1971, Hoxha, in a subtle but direct challenge, publicly expressed disagreement with China's foreign policy, including its new attitude toward Washington and its support for NATO and the Common Market.[21]

China's new foreign policy orientation represented a sharp divergence from the ideological approach to world affairs it pursued during the 1960s and ran counter to Albania's own stance. Although the U.S. threat to the Albanian regime had obviously receded, there was no corresponding change in Albanian perceptions of the U.S. menace. Ideologically, Hoxha found it difficult to accept that China, until then regarded as a socialist showcase, could "betray" Marxism-Leninism, the cause of proletarian revolution, and the national liberation struggle. But perhaps more importantly, Hoxha was concerned about the potential adverse effects of rapprochement with the United States on Albanian domestic policies. The success of his hard-line policy and social experimentation depended to a great extent on Albania's insulation from outside influence. He apparently feared that extensive contacts with the outside world might encourage domestic forces demanding much-needed socioeconomic reforms.

The cautious and gradual opening toward neighbors and selected Western European countries that Hoxha sanctioned after the invasion of Czechoslovakia were already having a destabilizing effect on the internal situation. By 1973 the leadership was confronted with growing domestic pressures for change. Hoxha was distressed with the open challenge to his policies by the nation's cultural, military, and economic elites. The leadership was faced with growing demands for a relaxation of party controls, greater internal reforms, an acceleration of the diversification of external relations, and a gradual disengagement from an alliance with the PRC. These developments coincided with a deterioration of Hoxha's health,[22] which apparently touched off a subtle but important jockeying for power among his closest associates. Concerned that the situation might get out of hand, Hoxha launched a series of purges resulting in the decimation of the top cultural, military, and economic echelons.

Following Nixon's visit to Beijing, Albania and China could no longer agree upon common goals, strategies, and tactics or coordinate activities toward those ends. But while defying China on several major issues, Hoxha was careful not to provoke a break with Beijing. Tiranë's external transactions were still highly concentrated toward the PRC, and Chinese assistance was essential to Albania's economic well-being. Prior to Mao Zedong's death in 1976, Hoxha continued to emphasize the importance Albania attached to its alliance with the PRC. At the same time, however, Albania embarked on a cautious, but significant, restructuring of its foreign policy and an internal belt-tightening policy. The Albanians made a concerted effort to reduce dependence on China by diversifying trade, diplomatic, and cultural relations, especially with Western European countries. In addition, the government began to stress the principle of self-reliance as the main element in the country's economic development. Hoxha institutionalized the idea with the inclusion of a provision in the 1976 constitution prohibiting the government from seeking foreign aid and credits or forming joint companies with foreigners.[23]

China, as had the Soviet Union in the late 1950s, appeared powerless to compel Albania to embrace its own foreign policy positions. It responded by gradually decreasing its foreign assistance and proceeding—much to Tiranë's chagrin—with the strengthening of political ties with Albania's neighbors, Yugoslavia and Romania.

With Mao's death in September 1976, Albanian-Chinese disagreements entered a critical stage. Hoxha was disappointed with the outcome of the post-Mao power struggle, apparently having supported the defeated radical faction. At the Seventh APL Congress in November 1976, Hoxha, in a clear affront to the Chinese, failed to endorse the post-Mao leadership headed by Hua Guofeng and vehemently criticized Beijing's pragmatic policy toward the United States and Western Europe.[24] In June 1977 it was reported that the rehabilitation of Deng Xiaoping, who had been dismissed in April 1976 and was publicly denounced by the Albanians, including Hoxha at the Seventh Congress, was imminent. In addition, Beijing announced that Tito had been invited to visit China—a personal insult to Hoxha, who had visited China only once, in 1956. Albania soon began its public propaganda barrage against China that, within a year, would lead to the disintegration of the Albanian-Chinese alliance. In July 1978 China terminated all economic and military assistance to Albania, recalled its specialists, and suspended trade ties, stopping short of breaking diplomatic relations with Tiranë.[25]

The break with China left Albania in an unprecedented situation, without a foreign protector or close friend. But for the first time in their modern history the Albanians could assert that their country was truly independent. Hoxha had taken steps to prepare the country for the break with China and minimize the adverse impact of the cessation of foreign assistance by having strengthened ties with neighboring countries and diversified external trade relations. Albania adopted a strategy of independent economic development. Hoxha made it clear that the rift with China would not result in Albania's alliance with another great power or military bloc.[26] The country continued to abide by the "dual-adversary" strategy, ignoring or rebuffing U.S. and Soviet calls for normalization of relations. Hoxha insisted that the PSRA was now the only real socialist state in the world. But this did not prevent Albania from expanding relations with neighbors, Western Europe, and the Third World.

DOMESTIC POLITICS

Hoxha had pursued a hard-line domestic policy, religiously guarding the party's monopoly over all aspects of Albanian society. He had refused to dismantle the Stalinist centralized system, although it had become obvious that political and economic institutions were malfunctioning. Nevertheless, colossal achievements were evident in many fields. Albania had become self-sufficient in the production of cereal grains, electrical energy, oil, and other chemicals, and had even become an energy-exporting country. Crash industrialization had resulted in the creation of a relatively strong industrial base and significant growth in real per-capita consumption. By guaranteeing job security and price stability (especially for basic commodities), eliminating taxes, and reducing wage differentials, the party had kept in check the population's aspirations. Hoxha, however, had pursued his strategy of economic growth, with gross imbalances in investments to benefit the development of heavy industry, at the expense of mass welfare.

Education and medicine had made quantum leaps. Illiteracy, a dominant feature of pre–World War II Albania, was reportedly eliminated, and there was a considerable reduction in the incidence of most infectious diseases. From the beginning of their rule, the Communist authorities had emphasized the necessity of raising the cultural level of the population. The rapid expansion of educational and occupational opportunities, especially for the previously unprivileged sectors of the society, helped strengthen the APL's popular support and legitimacy. But as was the case with the economy, education was subjected to rigid centralized planning, with the emphasis on vocational education and the training of technicians and skilled workers. In 1957 the University of Tiranë was established, which thirty years later had an enrollment of some 12,500 students. The Academy of Sciences was founded in 1972. The government had built an impressive network of professional and vocational schools. By the mid-1980s, more than 740,000 Albanians, out of a total population of three million, attended school at all levels, with a teaching staff of over 40,000 (Table 2.1).

Education and cultural development in general, however, were handicapped by restrictions on freedom. The authorities imposed strict censorship on the press, publishing, and the performing arts. All means of information and communication were put under state ownership, and the writers' union served as a supplemental instrument for the implementation of the APL's will. The authorities made sure that the educational system would serve the regime's ideological and political objectives, which included the education of the "new" man with appropriate communist traits, morality, and atheistic ideas, and the eradication of the remnants of the country's past "bourgeois" cultural traits. With the party controlling every facet of the school system, educational institutions had little say regarding programs, curricula, administration, and teaching staffs. Genuflections to the infallibility of the party's and, more specifically,

TABLE 2.1
Expansion of Education in Albania

	1938	1950	1960	1985
Pupils and students	56,300	178,000	311,500	743,700
High school students	1,700	6,800	29,900	661,700
Students completed higher institutes	NA	690	2,877	3,248
Teachers and instructors	1,551	5,423	10,874	40,828

Source: Adapted from Bardhyl Golemi and Vladimir Misja, *Zhvillimi i arsimit të lartë në Shqipëri* [The Development of Higher Education in Albania] (Tiranë: "8 Nëntori," 1987), pp. 40-41.

Hoxha's pronouncements on educational and cultural policy were obligatory.

The Albanian constitution guaranteed women equal rights with men in all aspects of life, including the family. The Communists inherited a situation in which women had a submissive status and were among the least advantaged in terms of social and economic development. From the outset, Hoxha emphasized the need to involve women in the country's economic development. Through a series of measures, including the well-coordinated campaign for the emancipation of women launched in 1967, the APL created favorable conditions to help women realize their full potential as human beings and contribute meaningfully to the sociopolitical development of Albania. In 1985 women accounted for 47 percent of workers and 51 percent in the education sector.[27] Their share of experts with higher education had steadily grown (Table 2.2). Increasing numbers of women were named to positions of responsibility and leadership in the economic and cultural sectors as well as in the government and the party.

Whatever yardstick was used, there was no doubt that under Hoxha's rule Albania experienced significant socioeconomic transformations. These gains, however, were overshadowed by Hoxha's legacy of repression. The Albanian government, insisting that human rights had a high status in the country, asserted that it respected the inviolability of individual freedom and dignity. But through overwhelming restrictions and controls on the population, Hoxha made Albania one of the most closed countries in Europe, with a dismal record on human rights. He created a system that attempted to close to its citizens every access to thought that was out of tune with official liturgy. Decades under Hoxha's rigid ideological mentorship had convinced the APL that it held a

TABLE 2.2
Women Specialists with Higher Education

Profession	1960	1970	1985
Engineers	5.8	10.6	20.8
Agronomists, veterinarians, and zootechnicians	6.6	3.7	20.2
Economists	17.1	17.8	50.1
Doctors and other medical workers	18.6	28.2	48.5
Teachers	25.3	26.4	43.4

Source: Bardhyl Golemi and Vladimir Misja, Zhvillimi i arsimit të lartë në Shqipëri [The Development of Higher Education in Albania] (Tiranë: "8 Nëntori," 1987), p. 170.

monopoly on truth. On the eve of Hoxha's death, Albania remained securely bound to an order of things already denounced in other communist countries.

Hoxha's isolationism, which denied Albania potential gains through greater external interaction, and the highly centralized management system he instituted retarded the country's technological development and relegated Albania to a position inferior to that of its neighbors. In fact, the economic gap between Albania and its neighbors had widened. It was thus questionable whether the terror, coercion, and the sacrifices and distortions imposed by Hoxha were worthwhile. It remained up to his successors to attempt to face up to the need for systemic reforms in an effort to tackle the causes and symptoms of Albania's economic, political, and social difficulties.

3

From Hoxha to Alia

After a lengthy illness, Enver Hoxha, the founder of socialist Albania, died on April 11, 1985, at the age of seventy-six. For more than forty years, Hoxha had overseen the domestic and foreign policies of this small but strategically important Balkan country—traditionally a tempting prize for any outside power with political and military designs in that volatile region. His imprint was evident in all aspects of the Albanian polity. Because the majority of Albania's three million people had never known another regime, Hoxha's death was a momentous event.

Two days later, Hoxha was succeeded by Ramiz Alia in what turned out to be a smooth and rapid transition. To most observers this came as no surprise, for Hoxha already had laid the groundwork for the transfer of power to Alia. But the preparation was not as orderly as the succession itself: It involved a dramatic reshuffling of top party and government officials, resulting in the climactic demise or forced retirement of a number of Hoxha's long-time associates and senior members of the leadership who had played a prominent role in the country's post–World War II political life.

MEHMET SHEHU'S DEMISE

Throughout the 1960s, the Albanian regime had enjoyed a remarkable political stability. Prime Minister Mehmet Shehu (1913–1981) was regarded as the second-ranking member of the leadership. A celebrated military commander in World War II, Shehu's primary power base was the military and the secret police, the Sigurimi. With his assistance, Hoxha had maintained a tight grip on society. Although there were reports going as far back as the war period that they disagreed over party and military policies, Hoxha and Shehu evidently remained on good terms and worked successfully together. Shehu never challenged Hoxha's role as first secretary of the party and supported him in many confrontations with internal and external, most conspicuously Yugoslav and Soviet, adversaries.

While Hoxha formulated the general policy course, it was Shehu who made sure it was loyally implemented even if it required resorting to unpopular and repressive measures. Through the use of the efficient Sigurimi, Shehu prevented the creation of an organized opposition and kept in check actual and potential pressures for the democratization of Albania's rigid social structure. He was merciless in dealings with party and government opponents. Even during the war he was regarded as the most ruthless of the Communist leaders, reportedly carrying out summary executions of opponents. He is said to have been especially brutal during the regime's campaign to extend its authority throughout the country immediately after the war and during the bloody purges that followed the break with Yugoslavia in 1948. During a meeting in the 1950s in Moscow, Shehu reportedly told Soviet President Anastas I. Mikoyan that "Stalin made two mistakes. First, he died too early, and second, he failed to liquidate the entire present Soviet leadership."[1] More than any other member of the ruling elite, the much-dreaded Shehu became identified with the regime's repressive policies, which had transformed Albania into a Communist citadel. He was unpopular, especially among the young and the creative intelligentsia, which almost exclusively blamed him for the repression and the lack of freedom of self-expression.

In addition to Shehu, other core figures of the leadership included Hysni Kapo (1915–1979), reputedly Hoxha's most trusted aide, Defense Minister Beqir Balluku (1917–1977?), and Minister of Internal Affairs Kadri Hazbiu (1920–1983), a relative of Shehu. Ramiz Alia, on the other hand, although closely identified with Hoxha, played a secondary role and was not considered a serious contender to succeed Hoxha until 1980.

The policy consensus that had characterized Albania's leadership after the break with the Soviet Union began to disintegrate in the early 1970s as disagreements with China and growing contacts with the outside world adversely affected the domestic political situation. The leadership evidently was divided on how to respond to growing domestic pressures for cultural liberalization, economic reforms, and a more realistic foreign policy posture. Hoxha was concerned about what he regarded as an open challenge to his hard-line policies and the assertiveness displayed by top officials in charge of the cultural, economic, and military sectors. In spring 1973 he dismissed Central Committee members and main advocates of cultural liberalization Fadil Paçrami, Todi Lubonja, and Agim Mero. Later that same year, Hoxha suffered his first major heart attack. Although reportedly only his family and the senior party and government officials were aware of the seriousness of Hoxha's health problem,[2] this development seems to have given rise to a debate and maneuvering among his colleagues in preparation for the eventual succession.

Hoxha was distressed with what he perceived as a dangerous decline of party control over the armed forces and growing signs of the military establishment's disaffection with his direction of both foreign and domestic policies. Evidently fearing a military putsch, Hoxha in 1974 dismissed Balluku, Chief of Staff Petrit Dume, and the head of the Political Directorate Hito Çako. Mehmet Shehu officially assumed the post of defense minister. A year later, Hoxha extended his purge to the economic sector. The main victims were Chairman of the State Planning Commission Abdyl Këllezi, Minister of Industry Koço Theodhosi, and Minister of Trade Kiço Ngjela. Hoxha accused them of distorting the party's economic policy, attempting to introduce "revisionist" economic reforms, expanding the bureaucracy, and sabotaging key economic sectors. Extensive changes in the party and government leadership continued throughout the late 1970s.

Hoxha's actions during the mid- and late 1970s reflected a man in a great hurry. His health deteriorated to such an extent that he was no longer able to deliver long speeches in public. He reportedly prerecorded the main sections of the report to the Seventh APL Congress in 1976 and subsequent major speeches.[3] Hoxha was anxious to lay the groundwork for the succession. He appears to have been guided by three main factors. First, and perhaps most important, he wanted an orderly transfer of power that would preserve the country's political stability. With the replacement of the top levels of the cultural, military, and economic establishments and the reimposition of a strict party control, he apparently had prevented the emergence of alternate power centers that could threaten the APL's dominant role in the society. Second, he was determined to take measures to perpetuate his hard-line policies. Aware of the major policy shifts that followed successions in other communist countries, he strove to institutionalize his policies in the hope that his successors would find it difficult to retreat from the "genuine Marxist-Leninist path" he had charted for Albania. The new constitution promulgated in late 1976 incorporated Hoxha's views on, among other issues, the leading role of the party, the pursuit of an independent foreign policy, and the principle of self-reliance. This was followed in the late 1970s and early 1980s by the publication of a series of memoirs, diaries, and books, in which Hoxha ostentatiously set forth his views on a variety of domestic and foreign policy matters.[4] Finally, Hoxha most likely was concerned about the future of his family after his passing from the scene. He and Shehu had shown no mercy for the innocent families and close relatives of former colleagues who had fallen in their disfavor. The question of what fate would befall his family must have caused Hoxha great consternation. The arrest of Mao Zedong's widow after her husband's death in 1976 could only have heightened his apprehension.

By 1980 Shehu still appeared to have the best chance of succeeding Hoxha. Balluku had already been purged, and Kapo, the third-ranking member of the leadership, had died in 1979. Shehu fared relatively well during the reshuffling of government officials in April 1980. Although he was relieved of his duties as minister of defense on the grounds of his "heavy responsibilities" as prime minister, Shehu was able to ensure Hazbiu's appointment as defense minister, while another relative, Feçor Shehu, became minister of internal affairs.[5] He therefore seemed to have a clearly established lead over any potential rival, including Alia, whose position in the leadership by this time had been significantly enhanced.

It is difficult to pinpoint exactly when Hoxha decided to rule out Shehu as his possible successor and give his support to the much younger Alia. This turn probably took place during the preparation of the Seventh Five-Year Plan (1981–1985)—the first five-year plan based entirely on domestic resources. On the eve of the Eighth APL Congress, held in November 1981, Hoxha and Shehu apparently clashed over priorities in domestic economic development and economic relations with the West. Hoxha rejected the first draft of the new economic plan submitted by Shehu.[6] In contrast to Hoxha, Shehu reportedly had advocated a real-location of resources away from heavy industry so as to boost the consumer-goods sector, effect an improvement in the system of prices, and stimulate economic interaction with the West. Shehu incurred Hoxha's wrath by reportedly neglecting his government responsibilities and delaying the preparation of his report to the Eighth APL Congress because of his preoccupation with writing a book on the world economic crisis.[7] Not only emerging policy differences with Shehu but also Shehu's advanced age, ill health, and lack of political finesse seem to have influenced Hoxha's decision against him.

Initially, Hoxha evidently attempted to lure Shehu into a "graceful" retirement. He sanctioned the publication of the first volume of Shehu's collected works, a privilege enjoyed by no living member of the leadership other than Hoxha. In the preface, Shehu was described as a "loyal" party leader and Hoxha was quoted as referring to him as "a talented and legendary general."[8] The same themes were reflected in an extolling review of the book by Alia. Again, no member of the leadership, with the exception of Hoxha, had ever been lauded in such profuse terms.[9] Hoxha also gave increasing responsibility for the day-to-day running of the government to Adil Çarçani, Shehu's deputy.

As Albania faced mounting social problems and economic slowdown in the wake of the termination of Chinese foreign assistance, Hoxha apparently decided that Alia was better equipped than Shehu to carry out the heavy responsibilities and burdens his successor would inherit. Hoxha, according to his wife Nexhmije, "had much faith in and deeply appreciated his close collaborator, Comrade Ramiz Alia, in whom he saw a revolutionary embodying the ability, courage, wisdom, and determination needed to carry forward the complete construction of socialism at the head of the Central Committee of the APL."[10] In contrast to Alia, Shehu was unpopular, unpredictable, and temperamental. Hoxha's wife, a prominent Communist in her own right, apparently also opposed Shehu: With Shehu in control, she could expect to play no significant role in the post-Hoxha era. Moreover, the animosity between Nexhmije Hoxha and Shehu's wife, Fiqret, director of the influential V. I. Lenin Higher Party School in Tiranë, may also have contributed to Hoxha's falling out with Shehu. On the other hand, Nexhmije Hoxha had long-standing ties with Alia, going back to the war period when the two worked together in the Communist Youth Organization. Of all the members of the leadership, only Kapo and Alia apparently enjoyed personal relations with Hoxha and his family.[11]

When Hoxha's subtle efforts to convince Shehu to voluntarily step aside failed, the first secretary stepped up the campaign to dislodge his former comrade-in-arms. He took advantage of the engagement of one of Shehu's sons to a young lady from a politically undesirable family to vilify Shehu. At a Politburo meeting on December 17, 1981, a month after Shehu had emerged from the Eighth APL Congress with seemingly much of his power intact, Hoxha succeeded in having all the participants, including Hazbiu, rebuke Shehu. The following day the leadership issued the astonishing announcement that the prime minister had committed suicide.[12] Shehu was succeeded by his deputy, Çarçani.

Hoxha now moved swiftly to undercut any potential opposition from within the military and security forces that had traditionally supported Shehu. He turned against Shehu's most prominent allies with gleeful alacrity. In an unprecedented, sweeping purge, Hazbiu, Feçor Shehu, Shehu's wife, Foreign Minister Nesti Nase, Minister of Health Llambi Ziçishti, and an undetermined number of senior army and security officers whose political fortunes were closely linked to those of Shehu were arrested. In addition, in November 1982 Haxhi Lleshi, president of the Presidium of the People's Assembly (the titular head of state), eleven cabinet members, and the head of the State Planning Commission were summarily dismissed.[13] Alia, in addition to keeping his party posts, replaced Lleshi. The campaign against Shehu and his supporters climaxed with Hoxha's stunning declaration in November 1982 that the late prime minister, one of his closest collaborators for more than three decades, had all along been a foreign spy working simultaneously for U.S., British, Soviet, and Yugoslav secret agencies. Hoxha linked Shehu with Balluku and other senior officials purged during the 1970s, claiming they were all part of the same plot to overthrow the first secretary.[14] Hazbiu, Feçor Shehu, and Ziçishti were reportedly executed, and Fiqret Shehu and Nesti Nase were each sentenced to twenty-five years in prison.[15] With the decimation of Shehu's faction, Alia had the succession firmly within his grasp. Hoxha would tell his French friend and consulting physician, Paul Milliez, that the succession had been settled and he could now die "peacefully."[16]

ALIA'S ACCESSION TO POWER

Although Ramiz Alia's role in Hoxha's settling of accounts with the Shehu faction remained a mystery, he emerged as the chief beneficiary of those extensive leadership changes. Born on October 18, 1925, in the northern town of Shkodër, Alia had joined the Communist-led National Liberation Movement as a teenager, becoming a party member in 1943. At the age of nineteen, he was appointed political commissar, with the rank of lieutenant colonel, of the Fifth Combat Division, which was dispatched to Yugoslavia in late 1944. According to Hoxha, the young Alia "led large units of the national liberation army for the liberation of Albania and for the liberation of the peoples of Yugoslavia."[17] Immediately after the war, Alia occupied leadership posts in the youth organization and in the Office of Propaganda and Agitation of the party's Central Committee. He moved through party ranks at a time of great domestic upheaval and party factionalism. At the First APL Congress in 1948, he was elected a member of the Central Committee. After completing advanced studies in 1954 in the Soviet Union,[18] Alia rose rapidly under Hoxha's patronage, serving as minister of education (1955–1958) and becoming a candidate member of the Politburo in 1956. Together with Shehu and Kapo, Alia accompanied Hoxha to the Moscow conference of eighty-one Communist parties in November 1960, where the APL first secretary denounced Soviet leader Nikita S. Khrushchev. He joined the Hoxha leadership's inner circles in 1961, when at the Fourth APL Congress he became a full member of the Politburo and a member of the party Secretariat. Throughout the 1960s and the 1970s, Alia acquired extensive experience in party matters as well as in the cultural and ideological sectors and played a prominent role in Albania's ideological campaign against Soviet, Yugoslav, and, later, Chinese "revisionism."[19]

Alia's political experience closely resembled that of Hoxha and his world outlook did not seem to differ much from that of his mentor. In his public pronouncements, Alia invariably echoed Hoxha's ideas on major foreign and domestic policy issues. In December 1979, in a major

speech on the occasion of the centenary of Stalin's birth, Alia offered
a tempestuous defense of the APL's Stalinist policies, which had come
under increased criticism both at home and abroad. Noting that the
APL was the only ruling Communist party in Europe that had not
repudiated Stalinism, Alia asserted that the attitude toward Stalin represented "a clear line of demarcation between Marxist-Leninists and
modern revisionists." He added:

> The enemies of communism frequently call us Albanians "Stalinists."
> Enslaved by their own slanders and fabrications against Stalin, they think
> that by describing us in this way, they are abusing and insulting us. But
> it is an honor for us Albanians that we uphold the teachings of Stalin,
> which are the teachings of Marxism-Leninism, that we are working and
> struggling for socialism and communism with that determination and
> courage with which Stalin worked and struggled. To the communists and
> people of Albania, Stalin was and is inseparable from the triumphant
> doctrine of the proletariat which has lit the way to the achievement of
> all our victories.[20]

Whereas throughout his career Alia showed remarkable talent for
surviving the many purges that swept the top party and government
echelons, he was not known as someone who publicly spoke his mind.
Nonetheless, many party members and particularly the creative intelligentsia believed Alia exerted a moderating influence on the leadership,
especially during periods of domestic convulsion.[21] Consequently, his
main power base was the central party apparatus, and his most loyal
allies were among the intelligentsia.

In early 1983 Hoxha increasingly limited his own political activity,
going into semiretirement. Alia, with impeccable party credentials and
with Hoxha publicly according him a proximity that he had denied to
other members of the ruling elite,[22] assumed the day-to-day administration
of the nation's affairs. The only member of the leadership to hold two
top posts, Alia traveled extensively, took Hoxha's place on major occasions,
and delivered authoritative policy statements. That the succession had
been decided well in advance of Hoxha's demise was confirmed by the
speed and smoothness of Alia's selection as party first secretary on April
13, 1985, only two days after Hoxha's death and before his funeral.[23]

Although personally picked by Hoxha to be his successor, Alia did
not have Hoxha's charisma and obviously wielded considerably less
power and authority than his mentor. Nonetheless, he had the advantage
of being more than "the first among equals" in the Politburo. During
the last years of Hoxha's life, Alia had played a preeminent role in the
governing of the country, which enabled him to build his authority.

Only Rita Marko (b. 1920) and Manush Myftiu (b. 1919) had served longer than Alia in the Politburo, both having been elected at the Third APL Congress in 1956. Neither of the two, however, was considered a serious contender for the post of party first secretary.

Prime Minister Çarçani emerged after Hoxha's death as the second-ranking member of the leadership. Born in 1922 in the southern district of Gjirokastër, Çarçani became a full Politburo member in 1961. His career had been strictly within the government: He had served as minister of mines and geology (1959–1965) and as Shehu's deputy (1965–1981), before becoming prime minister in January 1982. The two senior Albanian officials appeared to complement each other: Alia with his wide experience as the party's chief watchdog on political, ideological, and cultural affairs, and Çarçani with his long and distinguished record as a shrewd administrator.

The composition of the top leadership that Alia inherited in April 1985 differed substantially from that of a decade earlier. Of the fifteen full and candidate Politburo members, eleven had been elevated to that body after 1975, most of them owing their rise to power to Hoxha. Nine of them were representatives of the postwar generation of leaders and had gone through a political experience different from that of their senior colleagues. The majority had made their political careers after the break with the Soviet Union. Almost all full and candidate Politburo members selected after 1975 had alternated between party and government posts. In contrast to their more senior colleagues, the newcomers had a superior level of formal education, giving a strong technocratic cast to the post-Hoxha leadership. Four of the freshmen had previously headed the Ministry of Industry and Mines, and their elevation to the Politburo reflected the importance the leadership continued to give to the development of heavy industry.

Following the dismissal of high-ranking cultural, economic, and military officials in the 1970s, Hoxha had rejuvenated the leadership by naming to top positions relatively young people who had distinguished themselves as local and district administrators. In May 1975 Hekuran Isai (b. 1933) and Pali Miska (b. 1931) were selected as full Politburo members, and Llambi Gegprifti (b. 1942) and Qirjako Mihali (b. 1929) as candidate Politburo members.[24] Significantly, Isai and Miska became full Politburo members without passing through the candidate stage, as was the usual case. Evidently, Isai caught Hoxha's attention with his good performance as first district party secretary in Librazhd and Dibër. Miska, Gegprifti, and Mihali, all economists with wide experience in the industrial and mining sectors, had played important roles in the campaign against the purged senior economic officials and former Politburo members Abdyl Këllezi and Koço Theodhosi. The Seventh APL

Congress in 1976 confirmed the selection of Hoxha's four appointees. In addition, it elected two new candidate Politburo members: Lenka Çuko (b. 1938), an agricultural specialist who had distinguished herself as first party secretary in the Lushnje district, and Simon Stefani (b. 1929), a specialist in the oil industry and first district party secretary in Permet and later in Tiranë. None of them had had careers purely within the party, and their prior links with Alia were probably minimal.

Hoxha continued with the invigoration of the party leadership at the Eighth APL Congress in 1981 with the promotion of Çuko and Stefani to full membership in the Politburo and the selection of two new full members, Muho Asllani (b. 1937) and Hajredin Çeliku (b. 1927), and three candidate members, Besnik Bekteshi (b. 1941), Foto Çami (b. 1925), and Prokop Murra (b. 1921). As in the case of Isai and Miska in 1975, Asllani and Çeliku became full Politburo members without passing through the candidate stage. While there was no evidence of close links between Alia and Çeliku, who by profession was a mechanical engineer, Alia most likely was instrumental in the elevation to the Politburo of Asllani, Bekteshi, Çami, and Murra. The latter, with the exception of Bekteshi, had served as first district party secretaries in Shkodër, Alia's hometown. Both Asllani and Bekteshi were born in Shkodër. Alia's links with Murra were further strengthened after Murra's appointment to the party Secretariat in 1976. Professor Foto Çami had a long-standing association with Alia. A prominent member of the intelligentsia and of the prestigious Academy of Sciences, Çami, in contrast to his Politburo colleagues, saw his political career flourish rather belatedly. At the time of his selection as candidate Politburo member in 1981 he was fifty-six years old. An active participant in the partisan war, Çami joined the party in 1944 but did not become a member of the Central Committee until 1971, after having worked for many years in the Central Committee's Sector of Propaganda. He had also served as first district party secretary in Krujë and Tiranë, in addition to Shkodër.

Conveying a sense of continuity and stability, Alia moved gradually, but confidently, to strengthen his power and build his authority. In July 1985 Çami was appointed to the Secretariat, and the chairman of the State Planning Commission was replaced. Within a short period of time, Alia established a dominant profile in the official media and took over all the posts held by Hoxha, with the exception of that of head of the Democratic Front, the country's largest and most important mass organization. In March 1986 Hoxha's widow was named chairperson of the Democratic Front. With this decision, Alia gave Nexhmije Hoxha a position with high visibility but little power and may in fact have precluded the possibility of her appointment to a senior party or state post, including membership in the Politburo.

The Ninth APL Congress, which met in November 1986, confirmed Alia as the country's undisputed leader. Changes approved by the congress suggested that Alia's supporters dominated the Politburo and the Secretariat. The new Central Committee elected at the congress also reflected Alia's strength. Not surprisingly, Çami, Bekteshi, and Murra were promoted to full membership in the Politburo, thus filling the positions left vacant by the deaths of Hoxha, Shehu, and Hazbiu. Vangjel Çërava (b. 1941) and Pirro Kondi (b. 1923?), who in 1985 had replaced Çami as first party secretary for the Tiranë district, and Kiço Mustaqi, first deputy minister of defense and chief of the General Staff, were elected candidate Politburo members. The promotion of Murra to full membership and Mustaqi to candidate membership of the Politburo restored the military as an institutional voice in the highest party organ. Despite the rejuvenation of the top leadership, at the Ninth APL Congress the postwar generation had not yet replaced its predecessors. The old guard, consisting of Alia, Çarçani, Çami, Çeliku, Marko, Murra, and Myftiu, was still firmly in control.

ALIA: CHARTING A NEW COURSE

Alia inherited a country isolated from the outside world, with a largely dispirited and apathetic population, menacing economic and political troubles requiring adaptive responses, and—perhaps more important—one of the most secretive and doctrinaire Communist leaderships in the world. The economy suffered from a host of problems endemic to centrally planned economies: low productivity, permanent shortages of basic foodstuffs, an ailing infrastructure, and huge subsidies. By the mid-1980s social mobility for many segments of the population had slowed down and a new class had emerged, determined to hold on to power and preserve its privileges. The internal political situation appeared strained amid a deepening economic crisis, an apparent growing rift between large portions of the society and their rulers, and uncertainty about the future. Social malaise had become pervasive, and significant segments of the population seemed bent on rejecting established regime values. Economic difficulties as well as adverse social trends—most dramatically reflected in the increasing disintegration of social controls and self-discipline, which pointed to the waning hold of the official ideology—were beginning to undermine the social contract that had kept the Albanians politically quiescent throughout the post-1945 period.

Potential and actual pressures for change within the party, which in the past had been kept under control by Hoxha's threat or use of coercion, had been building up for some time. Rising leaders in the cultural, economic, and military sectors, like their predecessors in the early 1970s, were likely to exert pressure on the top leadership for greater autonomy in their respective domains. There appeared to be considerable discontent over the regime's failure to observe internationally recognized standards of human rights and inability to meet basic human and material needs. The state's formal abolition of institutionalized religion in 1967 was also apparently widely resented. Although official sources acknowledged a revival of "religious remnants and backward customs," there were no visible signs of organized opposition.

The intelligentsia, yearning for greater creative freedom, resented rigid party controls. Young people appeared to be alienated and disillusioned with the system and its ideology, and, to the consternation of party ideologues, highly susceptible to Western lifestyles, art, literature, music, and fashion. Many youths lacked what the authorities termed "communist convictions" and "socialist norms of conduct." Clearly, the APL had not succeeded fully in its efforts to instill in the population "appropriate" Marxist-Leninist attitudes.

Some foreign observers argued that because Alia was very much a product of Hoxha's repressive totalitarian system, he was not likely to depart from Hoxha's policies of isolation and repression, as such deviation might undermine the very institutional structures that had made his rise to power possible. Indeed, Alia appeared to be a true believer in the system he had helped create, and there was no evidence to suggest that he or any other member of the top leadership questioned or had serious doubts about the efficacy of the system. Nevertheless, five years after Hoxha's death, it had become apparent that Alia was not a prisoner of past policies and was indeed searching for new solutions to the nation's problems. He displayed a distinct political style with different priorities. Although perilously constrained by Hoxha's legacy, Alia began to put his own stamp on the country's politics, changing the tenor of both domestic and foreign policies. He indicated, however, that change would be carried out in an orderly fashion. His major dilemma appeared to be how to move away from the rigid policies of his predecessor without alienating party hard-liners and unleashing pent-up forces that would pose a danger to his hold on power. While insisting that Hoxha's "teachings" remained the foundation of the general foreign and domestic policy line of Albania, Alia practically ended his country's international isolation, initiated small but potentially significant economic innovations, and relaxed somewhat the party's tight grip on society.

Under Alia, Albania took diplomatic initiatives to break from its self-imposed isolation. He accelerated the process of diversifying the country's external relations, concentrating on stabilizing and strengthening

relations with Greece, Italy, and Turkey; finding a modus vivendi with
Yugoslavia and containing the adverse effects of the ethnic conflict in
Kosovë on Tiranë-Belgrade relations; and expanding ties with other
European and Third World countries, while simultaneously maintaining
a hostile attitude toward the two superpowers. Albania embarked on a
more pragmatic and active foreign policy. In a clear departure from
Hoxha's policy of shunning multilateral meetings, Albania participated
in the Yugoslav-sponsored Balkan Foreign Ministers Conference in February 1988. In addition, it established ties with West Germany and
upgraded its relations to the ambassadorial level with most Eastern
European countries. The Albanian leadership apparently recognized that
Hoxha's isolationist policies had caused the country considerable political
damage. Alia's policy of returning Albania to the mainstream of international politics was also motivated by economic considerations. If Hoxha
had used tensions with other countries to implement his orthodox
domestic policies, especially by fostering the atmosphere of a besieged
fortress and mobilizing the population against an alleged threat to the
country's independence, Alia saw the expansion of external interactions
as a means of helping Albania tackle its economic difficulties.

Alia's domestic policies were characterized by a mixture of conservative and reformist elements. He ruled out the possibility of fundamental, systemic reforms that held out the promise of overcoming the
stagnation, inertia, and backwardness caused by Hoxha's policies. Neither
did he loosen the country's rigid political structure, expose Hoxha's harsh
political legacy, or fill in the blank spots in Albania's turbulent post-
1944 history. Instead, Alia indicated that his objective was to gird the
party and the masses for significant changes that would revitalize the
economy. He stressed the need to face realities in the economic field
and, insisting that these were "unusual times" for Albania, called for
a "great leap forward."[25] After a remarkably frank recitation of the
various ills that plagued the economy, he summoned the country to
make major improvements in economic performance, giving priority to
meeting increasing consumer demands and raising the population's standard of living. At the Ninth APL Congress, Alia said the problems facing
Albania had become more difficult and complex and could no longer
be solved by "pre-industrial" methods of management. He criticized the
excessively centralized economic system and urged a decentralization of
the decisionmaking process.[26]

The new Albanian leader blamed economic difficulties on problems
accrued during the last years of Hoxha's rule, allowing the inference
that responsibility for many of the problems ultimately lay with Hoxha.
Subtly, but unmistakably, he questioned the wisdom of some past
economic policies. Alia moved toward a partial decentralization of state

economic management and a reform of prices in certain sectors. These measures were designed to improve the system's efficiency and meet the population's basic needs. They did not threaten the foundation of the Albanian system and therefore were not politically risky for Alia, although some of them represented a departure from Hoxha's approach.

Available evidence indicates that Alia did not share Hoxha's ruthlessness and paranoia. During the first five years of his rule, he stressed the use of persuasion rather than coercion in dealing with sociopolitical problems confronting his regime. He eased slightly the excessive restraints and controls on the population. Foreign travel restrictions were cut back, with growing numbers of Albanians permitted to visit their relatives abroad, mainly in Greece, Yugoslavia, and certain Western European countries. General amnesties announced in January 1986 and in November 1989 reportedly resulted in the release of many long-term prisoners. Increasing numbers of foreign tourists who visited Albania reported a relaxed atmosphere, with most official and unofficial Albanian interlocutors willing to engage in wide-ranging discussions. But despite the apparent relaxation of restrictions and the rise in tourism, Albania's contacts with the outside world remained strictly controlled because of fear that such interaction would expose the country to foreign, particularly Western, liberal ideals and (eventually) political leverage. During 1989 less than 15,000 foreigners visited Albania.[27]

Albania's international image continued to suffer as a result of Hoxha's bureaucratic-authoritarian rule. The brutality of his regime in repressing human rights had marshaled considerable world opinion against the country and brought home to the Alia regime the need for more sensitivity to foreign public opinion. The government attempted to repair its damaged reputation on human rights by tolerating a somewhat more permissive political climate, toning down its antireligious campaign, permitting expressions of religion at home, and even allowing prominent Albanian religious leaders from abroad to visit Tiranë. But although repression was not applied indiscriminately and on a massive scale as during Hoxha's era, Albania remained a police state. Repression did not diminish significantly, it merely became more subtle. The persecution of political opponents continued. Political participation remained limited, with nonparty groups having practically no chance to participate in the country's affairs, and the ruling elite's monopoly on power unshaken. The government appeared as determined as ever to suppress any signs of dissent. Arrest could still be arbitrary, due process minimal, and judgment severe. Moreover, there were few possibilities of domestic redress for gross abuses of human rights. The Albanian government, if it had become more sensitive to outside criticism, continued to display an intransigent position on the issue of human rights. In 1989 the United

Nations voted to appoint a rapporteur to examine the human rights situation in Albania.[28]

In the sphere of cultural policy, Alia displayed a degree of openness and toleration. Although he did not relax censorship, he encouraged public discussion of cultural, economic, and social problems. In a meeting with writers and artists in Korçë in August 1985, Alia called for a new standard of literature, sparking a lively debate and a plea for freedom of expression. In what appeared to be a move against the old-line establishment and the entrenched cultural bureaucracy, official media criticism chided prominent writers, critics, and editors for their "poor creative work." An editorial in the literary newspaper *Drita* in January 1986 noted that during discussions organized by the Union of Writers and Artists there had been "a general clash of opinions."[29] Another *Drita* editorial complained that "conformism and smoothing over differences hinder the expression of opinion, without which there can be no debate."[30] Dritero Agolli, chairman of the Union of Writers and Artists, in an uncharacteristic admission said that writers "lack creative courage." According to Agolli, "creativity without contradictions and serious problems has become a trend. This has hindered creative thought. . . . When one creates with the fear 'stop, maybe I was optimistic,' 'stop, maybe I was too pessimistic,' then one fails to achieve a deep realistic portrayal."[31]

Alia's own remarks on the question of the relaxation of cultural rigidity, however, were open to a broad interpretation. He called for promoting criticism and self-criticism and for creating "a favorable climate for as broad and as progressive a creativity as possible." But he also stressed that writers and artists should assist in achieving the goals of the APL.[32] Çami, who appeared more in tune with Alia's thinking on cultural affairs than did other Politburo members, urged the intelligentsia to engage in a free debate about various problems and to offer solutions. Speaking at a writers' meeting in Tiranë in February 1989, he said writers and artists should not hesitate to express their opinions for fear of making "mistakes."[33]

The debate among writers and artists, encouraged by Alia, was in sharp contrast with the past suppression of differing views and the APL's emphasis on conformity. Some officials, however, appeared to be out of sync with Alia. Stalwart conservatives opposed significant easing of the APL's political controls over cultural and intellectual life, fearing that cultural liberalization would lead to open dissent from the intelligentsia. Officials representing what was described as "narrow sectarian" views came under increasing attack. According to an article published in June 1987 in *Drita*:

There is no way to arrive at the objective truth without the confrontation and clash of opinions, tastes, and artistic viewpoints. Yet it is not seldom that presenting different opinions about artistic works, issues, and problems is taken as a threat to our general line and principles. In reality, in deep and serious discussion, even when opposing views are expressed, our general ideological line is not threatened. . . . And as soon as it appears that somebody has "stepped out of line," then attention is called to them, they are quoted as being in error, rephrased, and interpreted in different ways, down to ideological insinuations and disparaging remarks about critics in creative discussions and in the press. . . . Of course, in these cases it is not a question of criticizing the critics, but of a brake on creative debate and a poisoning of the atmosphere.[34]

The rhetoric in favor of change became louder and the regime relaxed its tight control over the country's cultural life. Literary orthodoxy began to be challenged by an increasingly outspoken intellectual elite. Without criticizing Hoxha by name, some writers began to examine the horrors of the former dictator's rule. Neshat Tozaj published a novel entitled *Thikat* [Knives], which denounced the brutality and absolute power of the dreaded secret police. Tozaj, himself an employee of the Ministry of Internal Affairs, tells the story of how the secret police falsified evidence, violated basic human rights, and arrested and imprisoned innocent people.[35] In a lavish review of the novel, Ismail Kadare, Albania's best-known writer, said Albanian writers had paid little attention to the violation of the law and human rights, adding:

These problems cannot be explained or skimmed over in stereotypical, cosmopolitan, rightist, or leftist formulas but must be confronted realistically and concretely. . . . The fact that *Thikat* will disturb the conscience of many people will prove its emancipating effect. A society that dares to denounce evil, that can exorcise it even if doing so is associated with painful things, as it is in the story told in this book, shows that this society is marching resolutely toward progress—a progress that no force in the world can hinder.[36]

At a literary conference in November 1989, Kadare sharply criticized the government's interference in literature. He said the writer should exercise his freedom to create without fear from the authorities, adding that no government can grant or deny the writer his freedom to create.[37]

In a significant departure from past practice, Alia also advocated an Albanian-style *glasnost* (openness) campaign, but kept it within carefully set limits. He insisted that "people should always be talked to openly, whether about their complaints or about difficulties and shortcomings."[38] In a message of greeting to the editorial board of the

party daily, *Zëri i Popullit,* on its forty-fifth anniversary, Alia sharply
criticized the role of the press in Albania. He called for a struggle
"against hollow phrases which seek to conceal poverty of thought,
against overblown euphoria which seeks to replace the analysis of facts,
against stereotypes and schematicism which illustrate poverty of imagination, and which unfortunately are not uncommonly encountered in
some press articles and in radio and television programs."[39] Meanwhile,
Çami, in a wholesale attack on the media's failure to provide timely,
objective, and comprehensive information to the masses, asserted paradoxically, "The strength of our propaganda lies in its truth." He added:

> The more frank we are with the masses, the more openly we talk, and
> the more honest we are with them, the better we present problems before
> the people and discuss them, the more responsible they then become for
> tasks that emerge and the stronger the ties between party and people
> grow. Let us give people more information both on domestic and foreign
> problems.[40]

Controversial articles appeared in the official media, which would
have been unthinkable during Hoxha's era. Sociologist Hamit Beqja
advocated an intensification of the "free debate," maintaining that debate
"stimulates, democratizes, and revolutionizes the country's entire life"
and serves as a guarantee against "fruitless doctrinaire thinking and
blind conformism."[41] Other scholars, echoing Alia's encouragement of
public debate, urged an expansion of cultural ties with other countries.[42]
But contacts with the outside world continued to be disfavored as
ideologically risky because of the alarming responsiveness of the Albanian
public to "foreign influences." Çami acknowledged that Albania's developing relations with other countries had led to an increase in what
he called "foreign ideological pressure." Although he recommended
vigilance, he said the only way to struggle against such pressure was
"through a democratic, free, and comradely discussion and debate."[43]

Alia received mixed responses from intellectuals, workers, and
upwardly mobile professionals to his calls for the reinvigoration of the
Albanian society. His program of economic changes rested on a narrow
popular base. The intellectuals were apparently most supportive of Alia.
Workers were generally apathetic because of Alia's inability to offer them
immediate and visible improvements in their daily lives: Alia's discipline
campaign resulted in their having to work harder for less pay because
of the recently established quality controls. The elderly, especially party
ideologues, seemed uneasy about Alia's policy, and the young largely
indifferent. But perhaps more important, many bureaucratic go-betweens
and party functionaries, fearing that their power and privileged positions

were being undermined, resisted the proposed changes. In their speeches, both Alia and Çami implied there were serious problems in changing the authoritarian style of party officials and managers. The old way of doing things simply could not be altered without breaking the stronghold of the party and government apparatus.

Although there appeared to be a leadership consensus on the urgency of reform, the measures Alia introduced did not represent an appropriate answer to the causes and symptoms of the country's social and economic difficulties. There was no debate about the future of the system or an admission that the political and economic institutions were malfunctioning. The changes Alia instituted, whereas significant in Albania's context, fell far short of the fundamental reforms needed to tackle the country's problems. Therefore, changes in the rigid internal system and an improvement of the regime's dismal record on human rights will most likely be slow. But greater contacts with the outside world and political upheaval in Eastern Europe have increased domestic pressures for internal liberalization. It was unlikely that Albania could indefinitely develop as an island politically separated from the rest of Europe. There was no doubt that Hoxhaism was on the way out; the question was not whether but when and how.

4

Government and Politics

Enver Hoxha left his successor a legacy of an authoritarian political system, with the APL holding a monopoly over political power, permeating all institutions of the state, and serving as the arbiter of truth. No Eastern European country had gone further than had Hoxha's Albania in copying the Stalinist political model and arbitrarily using political coercion and terror to deal with the country's political, social, and economic problems. While Hoxha deserved credit for Albania's significant economic and cultural development, this progress had been exacted at an enormously high human price. The military and the secret police had served as the mainstays of Hoxha's regime, providing an effective element of control over the population. He had carried the "class struggle" to an extreme, uprooting large sectors of the society. Thousands of "class enemies" were executed, imprisoned, or interned in labor camps, giving Albania the reputation of a police state.

In 1984 the London-based human rights organization, Amnesty International, published a comprehensive report on human rights violations in Albania, particularly political imprisonment, and described conditions in Albanian prisons and forced labor camps. Amnesty International expressed concern about the jailing of prisoners of conscience; legislation that severely restricted the exercise of internationally recognized human rights; breaches of international standards of fair trial; allegations of the torture and maltreatment of detainees, in particular during investigation proceedings; and the use of the death penalty. Noting that the Albanian government had not ratified either the International Covenant on Civil and Political Rights or the International Covenant on Social, Economic, and Cultural Rights and was not a signatory of the Final Act of the Conference on Security and Cooperation in Europe (Helsinki 1975), the report stressed that the constitution and legal provisions affecting human rights were conceived by the APL as instruments of "class struggle."[1] In January 1990, an American human rights organization, the Minnesota Lawyers International Human Rights

51

Committee, accused the Tiranë Government of suppressing freedom of religion, expression, movement and association.[2]

The Stalinist system had stunted the political growth and freedom of the Albanian people, stifled individual initiative, and distorted economic development. It remained up to his successors to ponder whether the positive aspects of Hoxha's rule, such as economic and cultural advances, the reduction of social inequalities, and guaranteed employment, could have been achieved with less social and human sacrifice and hardship, and through more humane means.

Whereas Eastern Europe had moved toward democracy, Albania remained what Nicholas C. Pano described as "the last bastion of Stalinism."[3] Even though the Stalinist political model was repudiated throughout the communist world and the former dictator was denounced anew in his homeland amid fresh revelations of the hideous crimes he had committed against his own people, the Albanian regime continued to idolize Stalin. Ramiz Alia's leadership seemed locked into an uninspiring Marxist-Leninist rhetoric, unable to significantly change the country's dilapidated system, with its ruthless security apparatus and moribund and seemingly unworkable economy.

Albania became perhaps the most outspoken and constant critic of Soviet leader Mikhail Gorbachev's *perestroika* (restructuring) and *glasnost* policies. Gorbachev's reforms were characterized as a continuation of Nikita S. Khrushchev's "revisionist policies." Self-styled as the world's only truly socialist state, Albania accused the Soviets of having "betrayed" Marxism-Leninism. The Albanians seemed particularly concerned about Gorbachev's economic reforms in the direction of a free market economy, gradual privatization of industry and agriculture, and acceptance of foreign investments. Of no less concern was the Soviet Communist Party's renunciation of its constitutional monopoly on power—an anathema to the Albanian regime. Although Alia insisted that the East European revolution would not affect his country,[4] Albania was not immune to political developments in Eastern Europe and the Soviet Union. In response to increased domestic and foreign pressures for change, in January 1990 the Central Committee announced a decentralization of party authority by enabling local organizations to appoint all but the most senior officials and experts. It also decided that basic party organizations hold "open" meetings, limited the term of office for many positions, and held out the prospect of putting forward more than one candidate for party and parliamentary elections. The Central Committee emphasized the APL's leading role in the society, adding that "the strengthening of the party must be a constant task, because the party is the country's leading force, with which the present and future of socialism and the country's freedom and independence are linked. The preservation of the leading role of the APL is a basic prerequisite for continuing socialist construction in Albania."[5]

Alia introduced some new features into Albanian politics, initiated potentially significant reforms in the economic sector, and permitted a degree of freedom of cultural expression—but the most repressive elements of Hoxha's bureaucratic-authoritarian system still remained intact. No measures were taken to reduce the APL's interference in economics and the legal system or to provide greater protection of individual rights. Although terror in the post-Hoxha period had gradually subsided, Alia's regime did not transcend the Stalinist traits of dogmatism, excessive centralization, insensitivity to the aspirations of the people, and pervasive controls over the society.

THE PARTY

Albania's constitution recognized the APL as "the sole leading political force of the state and of the society" and proclaimed Marxism-Leninism as the official and sole ruling ideology. The party's statute described the APL as "the leading force of the Albanian people." As the "vanguard" party of the working class, the APL gave "overall leadership to the working class in all aspects of the life of the country—political, economic, cultural, and military." The party had set as its immediate objective the complete construction of a socialist society and as its ultimate objective the creation of a communist society in which the principle "from each according to his abilities, to each according to his needs" would be applied.

Significant changes had been made in the party statute in the 1970s, after widespread political purges that resulted in the demise of senior leaders in charge of the cultural, military, and economic sectors, and in the wake of Albania's estrangement with China. Hoxha was determined to institutionalize his policies and apparently believed that by including appropriate provisions in the country's constitution as well as in the party's statute, the continuity of his policies would be ensured even after his passing from the political scene. The statute devoted particular attention to self-reliance, the class struggle, the prevention of the creation of factions within party ranks, and the struggle against "revisionism." With the gradual deterioration of relations with China, Hoxha, determined that Albania would not again become politically dependent on any other country, insisted on the strict implementation of the self-reliance policy. In line with Hoxha's notion of uninterrupted class struggle, the APL rules emphasized that a party member was required "to be a ruthless and courageous fighter against the class enemy, to wage the class struggle unhesitatingly and uninterruptedly."

Moreover, it stated that it was the duty of each party member to fight against any influence from "bourgeois and revisionist ideologies" as well as against "modern revisionism."

The APL operated on the principle of "democratic centralism," which provided for strict party discipline and the subordination of the minority to the majority. Theoretically, party members were guaranteed the right to freely express their opinions in meetings from the lowest to the highest bodies. But once a decision had been made with a unanimous or a majority vote, all party members were obliged to implement it "without further discussion." Decisions reached by the APL's higher bodies were obligatory for all lower bodies. Party organs were elected from the lowest to the highest and were required to report periodically to their party organizations and to higher bodies. The lowest level was the basic unit, consisting of at least three party members. Such units operated in factories, cooperatives, transport and construction enterprises, various institutions, and towns and villages. The basic unit recruited new members, administered local party affairs, and disseminated and implemented higher party directives. The APL had its central apparatus in Tiranë and was organized according to the country's territorial subdivisions. First party secretaries in the twenty-six districts wielded considerable political power.

The party statute emphasized that the APL did not allow "any kind of divisive or factional activity or any kind of deviation from its general line, from Marxism-Leninism."[6] Hoxha, however, had left his successors a legacy of party factionalism. The most critical periods in socialist Albania's history had been accompanied by sweeping purges. Stability through purges, including physical elimination of once-trusted associates, was one of the most distinguishable features of Albanian politics under Hoxha. The break with Yugoslavia in 1948 had resulted in the purge and subsequent execution of Koçi Xoxe, Politburo member and party organizational secretary. In the mid-1950s, as Hoxha came under increased Soviet pressure to reach an accommodation with Belgrade and launch a de-Stalinization campaign, Politburo members Tuk Jakova and Bedri Spahiu were dismissed. The Albanian-Soviet break claimed such prominent victims as veteran Communists Liri Belishova and Koço Tashko. But the most extensive purges occurred during the 1970s, when Politburo members Beqir Balluku, Koço Theodhosi, Abdyl Këllezi, and a number of senior officials were expelled. Hoxha used the dismissed officials as scapegoats for the country's problems, especially economic failures, invariably accusing them of sabotage, espionage, and antiparty activities. Many routed officials were reportedly forced to confess to monstrous crimes that all knew were completely fictitious. Overnight they became nonpersons, and their past contributions and roles in

Albanian politics were suppressed or ignored. The most preposterous charges were leveled against Mehmet Shehu, the former prime minister, and his closest associates. Shehu reportedly committed suicide in 1981 but subsequently was accused by Hoxha of being a spy for Yugoslavia, the Soviet Union, Great Britain, and the United States. Albania was the only socialist country in Europe where, as late as the 1980s, a dismissed Politburo member risked losing not only his privileges but also his life.

The highest body of the APL, as was the case with other ruling Communist parties, was the congress, which met every five years. Delegates to the congress were elected from district, regional, and city conferences. The functions of the congress, according to the party statute, were to examine and approve reports submitted by the Central Committee and other higher bodies, review and amend the party program and statute, determine the tactics of the country's domestic and foreign policy, and elect a Central Committee. The first APL secretary usually reported to the congress on the activities of the Central Committee and set the basic guidelines of the policies to be followed during the next four years, whereas the prime minister reported in considerable detail on the results of the previous five-year plan and submitted for approval guidelines for the country's economic and social development during the next five years.

Between congresses, the Central Committee directed party activities, administered funds, supervised lower-ranking bodies, and represented the APL in its relations with foreign communist parties and mass organizations. At its first meeting after a congress, the Central Committee elected the Politburo, the policymaking body of the party and the real locus of power, and the Secretariat, which was in charge of the day-to-day functioning of the party. The party statute provided that the Central Committee meet at least once in six months (although under Alia's leadership the Central Committee met on the average four to five times a year).[7]

The Ninth APL Congress, the first congress in the post-Hoxha era, convened in November 1986. It was attended by 1,628 delegates, 46.8 percent of whom were laborers, 21.1 percent peasants, and 32.1 percent white-collar workers. Women accounted for 24.4 percent of the delegates. Of the total number of delegates, 24.2 percent were from eighteen to thirty-five years old, 63.8 percent were between thirty-six and fifty-five, and 12 percent were over fifty-six years. More than half of the delegates, 54.9 percent, had completed higher education, 31.6 percent high school, and 13 percent eight years of elementary school.[8] The APL membership, which amounted to 122,600 at the Eighth Congress in 1981, had risen to 147,000 (Table 4.1). Workers accounted for 39.2 percent of the total membership, peasants 29.5 percent, and white-collar workers 31.3 per-

TABLE 4.1
Membership of the APL, 1948-1986

Year	Number
1948	45,382
1952	44,418
1956	48,644
1961	53,659
1966	66,327
1971	86,985
1976	101,500
1981	122,600
1986	147,000

Sources: The Academy of Sciences of the PSR of Albania, *Fjalori Enciklopedik Shqiptar* [The Albanian Encyclopedic Dictionary] (Tiranë, 1985), pp. 514-21; and *Zëri i Popullit*, November 4, 1986.

cent.[9] These figures reflected only a slight change in the social composition of the party's membership since the Eighth Congress. In 1981 workers had made up 38 percent of the total membership, peasants 29.4 percent, and white-collar workers 32.6 percent.[10] The composition of the Central Committee elected in 1986 reflected the leadership's determination to rejuvenate party cadres. A number of former members were not reelected because of their advanced age. The average age of Central Committee members was forty-nine years, compared with fifty-three years at the Eighth Congress. About 96 percent of the new members had completed higher education or had graduated from the V. I. Lenin Higher Party School. At its first meeting, the new Central Committee elected a Politburo, composed of thirteen full members and five candidate members, and a Secretariat, composed of five members.[11] During a government reshuffle in February 1989, the membership of the Secretariat was reduced from five to four secretaries (Table 4.2).[12]

Neither at the Ninth Congress nor in his subsequent pronouncements did Alia announce measures that would drastically change Hoxha's policies regarding the operation of the party and its leading role in the society. He called for "an uninterrupted class war" against internal and external enemies. But whereas Hoxha had emphasized the struggle against liberalism, his successor devoted greater attention to conservative, or sectarian, forces.[13]

In conjunction with criticism of sectarianism, Alia launched a campaign to streamline the bureaucracy and improve the work of party

TABLE 4.2
APL Politburo and Secretariat, 1989

Full Politburo members	Candidate Politburo members	Secretariat
Ramiz Alia	Vangjel Çërava	Ramiz Alia (First Secretary)
Muho Asllani	Llambi Gegprifti	Foto Çami
Besnik Bekteshi	Pirro Kondi	Lenka Çuko
Foto Çami	Qirjako Mihali	Hekuran Isai
Adil Çarçani	Kiço Mustaqi	
Hajredin Çeliku		
Lenka Çuko		
Hekuran Isai		
Rita Marko		
Pali Miska		
Prokop Murra		
Manush Myftiu		
Simon Stefani		

Sources: *Kongresi i 9-të i Partisë së Punës të Shqipërisë* [The Ninth Congress of the Albanian Party of Labor] (Tiranë: "8 Nëntori," 1986), pp. 383-84; and *Zëri i Popullit,* February 3, 1989.

cadres. The substantial increase in the number of people working in the central party and government administration had apparently become a serious economic burden. Moreover, middle-level bureaucrats, fearing the loss of their privileges and power, were evidently hampering the implementation of new policies, especially in the economic sector. Alia demanded a higher standard of cadre training and performance, adding that the country could not tolerate a situation "in which those who are incapable and sluggish remain in charge of work, because they hinder its development and progress."[14] An editorial published in April 1988 in the party daily pointed out that

> there are cadres who first rack their brains over how to escape problems, how to avoid self-sacrifice, and how to evade long periods of service in remote districts or backward enterprises and agricultural cooperatives where their assistance, ideas, and work are required. They simply kill time. They shut themselves up in their offices and try to ingratiate themselves with their chiefs with "Yes, sir! No, sir!" and "Your instruction will be carried

out at once!" but in reality they deal with trifles and do not tackle the main problems of daily life.[15]

The Politburo ordered that cadres in sensitive positions open to graft be rotated on a regular basis. It was conceded, however, that "movement in this direction is still slow, too little is being done, and in some cases it has become acceptable to make a lot of noise about this problem, while there is very little action."[16]

THE STATE

In 1976 the Albanian People's Assembly approved a new constitution, replacing the one adopted in 1946 and revised in 1950. Drafted by a constitutional commission headed by Hoxha, the document changed the official name of the country from "People's Republic" to "People's Socialist Republic." Albania was described "as a state of the dictatorship of the proletariat, which expresses and defends the interests of the working people." The constitution sanctioned the one-party system. In contrast with other socialist states, the first secretary was designated as the commander-in-chief of the armed forces and the Defense Council, thus underscoring the party's determination to hold the military under firm control and prevent it from attaining an autonomous position from which it potentially could challenge the APL. The document characterized the defense of the country as "the highest duty and the greatest honor" of every citizen and declared it an act of treason for anyone "to sign the surrender of Albania or to accept the occupation of the country" (Article 90). In line with Tiranë's independent foreign policy, the stationing of foreign troops or the establishment of foreign bases on Albanian territory was forbidden.

Officially described as the constitution of "the complete construction of the socialist society," the document embodied Hoxha's views on major policy issues. Private property was abolished and the economy designated as "a socialist economy." The government was prohibited from granting concessions to "capitalist and revisionist monopolies and states," forming joint economic or financial enterprises with foreign companies or countries, or seeking and obtaining foreign loans and credits. In addition, the new constitution reaffirmed the regime's 1967 decision to abolish institutionalized religion. According to Article 37, Albania would "not recognize any religion and supports and develops atheist propaganda." The document prohibited the creation of religious, fascist, and what it described as antidemocratic orgnizations.

The constitution guaranteed Albanian citizens certain inalienable rights, including freedom of speech, press, organization, association, assembly, and public demonstration (Article 53). Moreover, it protected the inviolability of the person and the home, and the privacy of correspondence (Articles 56–58). Whereas the list of these rights was impressive, the reality was different, with Albanians enjoying only limited political and civil freedoms. The constitution stressed that citizens could not exercise their rights "in opposition to the socialist order." And the penal code contained enough provisions to provide a legal basis for suppressing any signs of dissident opinion.

The People's Assembly, according to the constitution, was the legislative branch of the government and the supreme organ of state. The 250 members of the assembly were elected from a single list of Democratic Front candidates for a term of four years. In the February 1987 elections, it was officially announced that all registered voters—1,830,653 of them—had participated in the election and not one had voted against official candidates. One ballot was found to be void.[17] The assembly met twice a year and served mainly as a rubber stamp to approve decisions already made by the Politburo. The fifteen-member Presidium of the People's Assembly acted on behalf of the assembly between sessions. The chairman of the Presidium was the country's titular head of state—a position held by Alia since 1982.

The Council of Ministers, appointed by the People's Assembly, was the executive branch of the government. It was in charge of the country's social, economic, and cultural activities. In 1990 Adil Çarçani, who had succeeded Shehu in January 1982, still held the post of the chairman of the Council of Ministers. Government at the district, regional, and city levels operated through people's councils. Elected for a three-year term, people's councils were charged with administering all the affairs of their geographic areas. The councils met twice a year. Between sessions, the councils' work was carried out by their executive committees. The Supreme Court was the country's highest judicial organ, and its members were elected by the People's Assembly. Albania had abolished its Ministry of Justice in the 1960s and the Office of the Prosecutor General supervised the implementation of the country's laws. In 1983 the Office of Investigations, which was charged with investigations into penal acts, was placed under the direct supervision of the Presidium of the People's Assembly. It was separated from the Ministry of Internal Affairs in order "to increase the objectivity" in its functions. Mehmet Shehu and former ministers of Internal Affairs Kadri Hazbiu and Feçor Shehu were criticized for misusing the Office of Investigations.[18] In practice, the courts enjoyed little independence. At a meeting of the Presidium of the People's Assembly in May 1985, Alia denounced outside interference in the investigative process and in court proceedings. Such interference, he said, was harmful for the party line.[19]

TABLE 4.3
Composition of the Albanian Government, 1989

Name	Title
Adil Çarçani*	Prime Minister
Pali Miska*	Deputy Prime Minister and Minister of Agriculture
Manush Myftiu*	Deputy Prime Minister and Chairman, State Control Commission
Simon Stefani*	Deputy Prime Minister and Minister of Internal Affairs
Enver Halili**	General Secretary of the Council of Ministers
Besnik Bekteshi*	Minister of Industry and Energy
Hajredin Çeliku*	Minister of Transportation
Reis Malile**	Minister of Foreign Affairs
Prokop Murra*	Minister of Defense
Niko Gjyzari**	Chairman, State Planning Commission
Andrea Nako	Minister of Finances
Vito Kapo**	Minister of Light Industry
Jovan Bardhi**	Minister of Food Industry
Farudin Hoxha	Minister of Construction
Osman Murati	Minister of Domestic Trade
Shane Korbeci**	Minister of Foreign Trade
Xhemal Tafaj**	Minister of Communal Economy
Skender Gjinushi	Minister of Education
Ahmet Kamberi	Minister of Health
Alfred Uçi	Chairman, Committee for Culture and Arts
Ajet Ylli**	Chairman, State Committee for Science and Technology

* Member of the Politburo
** Member or candidate member of the Central Committee
Source: Zëri i Popullit, February 21, 1987, and February 3, 1989.

Although the constitution granted the People's Assembly consider-able powers, the composition of its presidium as well as that of the Council of Ministers was decided by the Politburo. In addition, the chairman of the Council of Ministers (the prime minister), his deputies, and ministers in charge of the most important ministries were usually members of the Politburo. In 1989, seven of the twenty-one members of the Council of Ministers were members of the Politburo, and eight were members or candidate members of the Central Committee (Table 4.3). In no other Eastern European country did the ruling Communist party supervise government work to such an extent as did the APL in

Albania. Although Alia did not institute measures to separate the functions of the party and government organs, at the Eighth Plenum he complained that the party apparatus exercised overwhelming authority over government bodies. He spoke out against APL members' monopolizing management and administrative posts and stated that party membership should not be a prerequisite for appointment to government positions, including posts at the ministerial level. He said there was a need "to rely more and more strongly on the views of the masses regarding the appointment of cadres, and to abandon certain unnecessary rules involving the *nomenklatura* in the state apparatus, replacing them with open competitions for appointing people to certain posts and categories of work."[20] No doubt reducing the party's overwhelming power and separating government bodies from business enterprises would increase efficiency and cut bureaucratic impediments to the conduct of business.

MASS ORGANIZATIONS

In 1990 less than 4 percent of Albania's total population were members of the APL. To achieve its objectives the party relied heavily on mass organizations. The Democratic Front, successor to the National Liberation Front, was the party's most important auxiliary. This mass political organization, totally subordinated to the APL, was chaired in 1990 by Hoxha's widow, Nexhmije, a member of the Central Committee. The Democratic Front was the country's broadest mass organization and served as a school for mass political education. As an umbrella organization for cultural, professional, and political groups, the Democratic Front was open to all citizens eighteen years and over. Its main tasks and objectives were to strengthen the political unity between the party and the people and to mobilize the masses for the implementation of the APL's policies. As an instrument of the party, the Democratic Front nominated and campaigned for candidates for local and national elective posts. The list of candidates, however, was approved by the party.

The Union of Albanian Women was also considered an important instrument that helped the party control and supervise the political and social activities of women. The union, headed in 1990 by Lumturie Rexha, a member of the Central Committee, had played an important role in spearheading the party campaign for the emancipation of women. The APL had made considerable strides in securing equal social and political rights for women. They had become active participants in the political, economic, and social life of the country. They held responsible posts in the party (including the Politburo) and the government and had entered all the professions. By the mid-1980s, women accounted for 47 percent of the working force, about 30 percent of deputies in the

People's Assembly, 32 percent of party members, 30 percent of members of the Supreme Court, and 41.2 percent of the leaders of mass organizations.[21] But despite these significant advances, women in some parts of the country apparently still had a long way to go in achieving full equality with men. Moreover, officials complained that women were often assigned difficult tasks and that not enough attention was devoted to their working conditions, especially in the agricultural sector, where they accounted for 52 percent of the work force.[22]

The main tasks and objectives of the United Trade Unions of Albania, founded in 1945, were to carry out political and ideological education of the work force, maintain high morale among the country's laborers, and fulfill party directives. Unlike its counterparts in other countries, the United Trade Unions of Albania was less concerned with safeguarding the interests of the workers and more with ensuring the transmission of the party line to the workers and mobilizing support for the implementation of party guidelines. The union operated under the principle that the interests of the state and those of the workers were the same. Nevertheless, at the Tenth Congress of the Trade Unions, in June 1987, Sotir Koçollari, president of the union's general council, complained about management delays in solving workers' problems. He said there was "formalism in consulting laborers' opinions. Pledges and initiatives are not always supported by the administration, as there is not always a response to workers' suggestions, and changes are made in plans without consultation with workers." Koçollari said that only a fraction of "thousands of valuable suggestions" put forward by workers were accepted by the management. He also called for the revision of "some regulations, instructions, and norms" that hindered workers' initiative and whose time had "past."[23] An alarming increase of "antisocial" behavior, including theft of social property, corruption, and violation of labor discipline, apparently reflected workers' growing disillusionment with official values and disintegration of social controls and self-discipline.

The Union of Albanian Working Youth, founded in 1941, was a nationwide bureaucracy, its most basic function the ideological education of youth. Membership in the youth organization was often a prelude to membership in the APL and a ticket to academic and professional advancement. The youth organization operated under the direct leadership of the party's Central Committee and was considered one of the most active auxiliaries of the APL. In addition to disseminating and implementing party directives, the youth organization played an important role in the country's economic affairs, organizing special labor brigades to work on important construction projects.

During the 1980s, youth alienation and high susceptibility to foreign ideas and values and what officials termed corrupting influences presented a particularly tough challenge to the youth organization. Many young people had apparently become more attentive to what the outside world could offer them in material ways and ideas than they were to the strictures of Marxism-Leninism. The APL leadership expressed concern about what it believed to be a decline in moral standards among the country's youth.

Alia's government devoted considerable attention to the problems of the country's restless youth, a task that required great imagination and foresight, as Albania had one of the youngest and fastest-growing populations in Europe. By the mid-1980s, the average age of the population was 25.7 years, and 33.9 percent of the total were under fifteen years of age. In an uncharacteristic admission in March 1984, the party theoretical organ conceded that there had been an erosion of discipline among the young and an increase in such pathological social phenomena as parasitism, social anomie and low productivity, unwillingness to accept assignments in the countryside and remote areas, manifestations of religious belief, hooliganism, theft, and crime.[24] An Albanian official told a visiting Western journalist in June 1985 that the regime did not promote tourism—a potential source of badly needed hard-currency earnings—because of its fear "that our youth could be negatively influenced by foreign customs."[25]

The official media blamed the spread of "alien manifestations" among the youth on the influence of foreign radio and television broadcasts, remnants of "petit bourgeois mentality," and liberal attitudes on the part of schools and teachers.[26] The Union of Working Youth became the object of severe criticism for insufficient work with young people.[27] Whereas some officials advocated a strict approach in dealing with those influenced by foreign "ideological diversion,"[28] the media published articles urging that more understanding be shown to young people's needs and demands. Sociologist Hamit Beqja called for a more subtle approach in work with the country's youth and rejected the use of "administrative" methods. In a rare analysis of generational problems in Albania, Beqja said the older generation often did not have a clear understanding of the needs and aspirations of young people. He warned that administrative measures were likely to further alienate the youth:

It may seem that the administrative method solves everything, but this is a mistake, especially in relations with young people who are sensitive and impressionable or whose self-respect has been injured or who have "a mind of their own." It is possible that the "wound" may be suppressed inside, but not cleansed, and it can break open later even more strongly and with even more virulence.[29]

He denounced what he called conservative taboos inherited from the past and outmoded and bureaucratic practices and patterns of thinking, which "impoverish young people's lives and hamper their education and revolutionary maturation."[30]

In a major speech in May 1988, Mehmet Elezi, then first secretary of the Union of Working Youth, implied that an increasing number of young people were alienated from the youth organization because of strict limits on debate. He said, "The organization's word will carry weight when it addresses itself to problems that matter to young people and when it speaks in young people's language, fresh and well argued."[31] In autumn 1988 it was announced that special "social control groups" had been created in enterprises, agricultural cooperatives, schools, military units, and social facilities to tackle problems of "alien manifestations" among young people.[32] These measures, however, were not likely to solve the problem. What the youth appeared to need was the affirmation of its rights to a greater degree of free speech and free association, something that Alia apparently was not willing or ready to do. Nevertheless, while the APL continued to retain tight control over the youth, Alia had relaxed somewhat political controls over their lives.

CONCLUSION

As Albania entered the last decade of the twentieth century, Ramiz Alia faced the dilemma of dismantling the despotic and overcentralized regime inherited from Hoxha. Any attempt at introducing significant political reforms, however, would undermine his position by exposing him to criticism from conservatives that he was straying from Hoxha's course. Although he insisted on greater supervision of public officials and on reducing their opportunities to engage in corrupt practices, Alia did not confront the party's history, redress Hoxha's abuses, or take apart the many elements of the country's rigid political and economic system. The Albanian regime made no effort to introduce democracy within the APL by providing more free debate within its ranks and freer elections of party officials, restoring the primacy of elected party organs over the party apparatus, or permitting mass organizations to play a greater role in the Albanian polity. The regime also refused to take measures to devolve wide-ranging powers from the APL and state bureaucracy to the popularly elected legislature. Although Alia advocated multicandidate elections for lower party organs, the APL was slow in instituting electoral reforms.[33] A democratization of the election process, such as public discussion of candidates for office and the introduction of multiple candidacies, would undermine the *nomenklatura* system, which had allowed party leaders to impose their candidates from the top down.

The Albanian political apparatus lacked a system of checks and balances. There were no structures dividing authority among various segments of society, and the APL continued to wield too much power. No doubt, introducing diversity to the management of the nation's affairs would bring more creativity and would make it more difficult for wrong policies to be adopted or corrupt officials to rule. Political reform in Albania is likely, however, to lag far behind economic reform because it will involve reducing the power of entrenched organizations and individuals. Those in influential positions are likely to fight such efforts. Even if the economic decisionmaking process is decentralized, as Alia indicated, the APL will probably retain ultimate political control.

5

The Economy

No issue seems to have preoccupied the post-Hoxha leadership more than the economy, particularly the gargantuan task of reversing the effects of decades of mismanagement that by the late 1980s had led to a sluggish economic performance. The APL had relied on the Stalinist model of rapid industrialization. Hoxha's regime had sought to boost the living standards of the population in return for political obedience. During the more than four decades of Communist rule, Albania built an industrial base, and living standards, especially compared with the pre–World War II era, rose dramatically. These gains, however, were accompanied by a significant increase in popular aspirations for a freer and more abundant life. By 1990 the ability of the government to reach these goals had declined considerably. Following sizable gains during the two previous decades, in the 1980s Albanian living standards stagnated and opportunities for social mobility declined, mainly as a result of the government's decision to abide by the self-reliance policy following the cessation of foreign assistance from China in 1978. The Communist regime found itself in the precarious position of having to concede that it was unable to meet the population's basic material needs. As Albania entered the last decade of the twentieth century, it had become quite obvious that a further deterioration in economic performance would be politically untenable for the Albanian leadership.

ECONOMIC ACHIEVEMENTS AND DIFFICULTIES

Albania had a history of dependence on foreign assistance. As was the case during King Zog's era, in the post-1945 period Tiranë's economic policy closely followed its alliance pattern. Between 1945 and 1978, Albania ran a continuous balance-of-payments deficit, which was covered by assistance from Yugoslavia (1945–1948), the Soviet Union (1948–1961), and China (1962–1978). Thanks to substantial foreign assistance, the government was able to pursue its ambitious policy of rapid in-

TABLE 5.1
Sources of National Income
(in percentages)

Sector	1960	1970	1985
Industry	18.6	28.2	43.3
Agriculture	37.6	34.2	34.6
Construction	6.5	7.1	7.2
Transportation and trade	37.3	30.5	14.9

Source: Bardhyl Golemi and Vladimir Misja, Zhvillimi i arsimit të lartë në Shqipëri [The Development of Higher Education in Albania] (Tiranë: "8 Nëntori," 1987), p. 180.

dustrialization, which was aimed at making the country economically self-sufficient in as many fields as possible. Foreign aid, however, meant high political costs, a serious compromise of decisionmaking autonomy, and, in the case of the alliance with Yugoslavia, a near loss of independence and sovereignty. Thus the Albanian economy, perhaps more than any other Eastern European economy, had to operate under politically imposed constraints. Hoxha gave top priority to the restoration and preservation of the country's political independence at the expense of all other factors, including more rapid economic development.[1]

The APL was justifiably proud of the economic progress Albania had achieved under Communist rule. The regime's rapid industrialization policy had led to the creation of a relatively modern multibranched industry, which by 1985 was generating more than 40 percent of the total national income (Table 5.1). The government had given priority to the exploitation of the country's considerable natural resources such as oil, chrome, copper, iron, and hydropower. In 1984 alone, the Albanian economy produced more than two million tons of coal; 960,000 tons of chromium; and more than one million tons each of iron and nickel.[2] By the end of the 1980s, Albania was processing domestically most of its minerals—and producing its own machinery and industrial equipment, including complete factories and plants as well as Albanian-brand tractors. The engineering industry reportedly met 95 percent of the country's needs for spare parts. Albania had also become an energy exporter, selling oil, petroleum products, and hydroelectric power. Electrification of the entire country was completed in 1971, and with the inauguration of hydroelectric power stations in Fierzë and Koman, Albania began to export electricity to all its Balkan neighbors. The government had also made significant strides in improving the skills of the labor force. In

TABLE 5.2
Specialists with Higher Education

Profession	1970	1980	1985
Engineers	3,491	9,438	11,815
Agronomists, veterinarians and zootechnicians	1,768	6,042	8,584
Doctors and pharmacists	2,071	5,141	5,875
Economists	1,820	6,533	9,622
Teachers	4,537	16,069	19,967
Others	1,513	4,328	5,740

Sources: Vladimir Misja, Ylli Vejsiu, and Arqile Bërxholi, Popullsia e Shqipërisë [The Population of Albania] (Tiranë, 1987), p. 271; Bardhyl Golemi and Vladimir Misja, Zhvillimi i arsimit të lartë në Shqipëri [The Development of Higher Education in Albania] (Tiranë: "8 Nëntori," 1987), p. 177; and Directory of Statistics, The State Planning Commission, 40 Years of Socialist Albania (Tiranë, 1984), p. 47.

1985 there were 61,603 cadres with higher education. Of these, 11,815 were engineers and 9,622 economists (Table 5.2).

Substantial advances were also recorded in agricultural production. The APL claimed Albania had achieved the stage of development of an agricultural-industrial country and was on the way to becoming an industrial country with an advanced agriculture. In 1988 two-thirds of the population lived in the countryside, and 700,000 people were employed in the agricultural sector.[3] Large-scale programs of land reclamation, soil improvement, and irrigation; the introduction of new farm techniques and mechanization; and increased use of fertilizers had contributed to a significant expansion and modernization of agricultural production. In 1976 Albania declared it had become self-sufficient in bread grains.

Albania had gone further than any other Eastern European state in almost entirely socializing agriculture. More than 80 percent of the cultivated area was in the hands of collective farms, and 18 percent in the hands of state farms. A collective farm was considered the property of the particular collective or group of workers, whereas a state farm was the property of "the entire people," with its managers and workers entitled to guaranteed state salaries. During the last years of his reign, Hoxha had embarked on a policy of totally phasing out private plots and transforming collective farms into state farms. The authorities continued to allocate enormous resources to the agricultural sector. During the Seventh Five-Year Plan (1980–1985), about 30 percent of the total volume of investments was used for the development of agriculture.

In the Eighth Five-Year Plan (1986–1990), 32 percent of total investments were allocated to the agricultural sector.[4] Nevertheless, agriculture had become a problem sector of the economy, consistently failing to meet planned targets. The authorities apparently were never able to overcome the resentment that Hoxha's violent, all-out assault on peasant agriculture—in the form of full collectivization, completed in 1967—and reduction of private plots had caused in the countryside. In addition, agricultural production continued to be hindered by the persistence of traditional agricultural methods, low level of mechanization, and, perhaps most important, lack of material incentives.

The economy grew at a relatively rapid rate until the mid-1970s. The reduction of Chinese assistance, following the Sino-U.S. rapprochement in 1972, had an immediate, adverse impact on the Albanian economy. Plan objectives for the period between 1971 and 1973 were not met, and the completion of important projects was postponed.[5] Economic difficulties gave rise to disputes within the leadership on the country's economic strategy. In 1975 Hoxha purged the higher echelons of the economic establishment who had questioned some of the basic principles of his economic policy and had advocated the decentralization of the planning system and expansion of trade and cooperation with other countries, particularly Western European ones. In preparation for the eventual break with China, Hoxha, claiming that political independence could not be ensured without achieving economic independence, resorted to a strategy of independent economic development based on self-reliance. He institutionalized this strategy in the constitution promulgated in 1976. Article 28 stated:

> The granting of concessions to, and the creation of foreign economic and financial companies and other institutions or ones formed jointly with bourgeois and revisionist capitalist monopolies and states as well as obtaining credits from them are prohibited in the People's Socialist Republic of Albania.[6]

Within years of the break with Beijing, Albania's economy was on the road to recovery from the shocks of the cut in Chinese aid. But the policy of self-reliance turned out to be a disastrous failure. Judging the economy's performance against the APL's own standard,[7] the results were disappointing. There was a significant decline in industrial production, particularly in the extraction of oil and production of electricity— two highly important sources of hard-currency earnings. The exploitation of natural resources was hampered by obsolete machinery and equipment, a lack of technical expertise, poor organization, and an inability to fully assimilate imported technology. Albania appeared to be particularly in need of updating equipment in the mining and oil industries in order to exploit fully its reserves of chrome, nickel, copper, natural gas, iron, coal, lignite, and oil. Even as late as 1986, projects were based on outmoded technology.[8] Low foreign reserves and constitutional restrictions on foreign loans and credits limited the country's technology imports. Moreover, during the mid- and late-1980s, exceptionally severe winters and prolonged droughts further aggravated Albania's economic difficulties.

At the Ninth APL Congress in November 1986, Alia disclosed serious shortfalls in the leading sectors of the economy during the period of the Seventh Five-Year Plan (1980–1985). Industrial production, targeted to increase by 36 to 38 percent, grew by 27 percent. The performance of the agricultural sector was especially poor: Instead of the projected increase of 30 to 32 percent, production went up by only 13 percent. Considerable problems were reported in the oil, gas, mining, and machine industries, leading to a shortage of goods for export. Particularly disappointing were the figures for exports, which grew by 29 percent instead of the planned 58 to 60 percent.[9] Although they blamed "objective" factors—bad weather, prolonged drought, earthquakes and floods, and the negative influences of the world economic crisis—for many of the deficiencies, Albanian officials also criticized "failures in organization and management of labor, bureaucratic attitudes, and liberal and technocratic manifestations."[10]

Most targets for the Eighth Five-Year Plan (1986–1990), in comparison with the 1980–1985 plan, were scaled down. Nevertheless, based on the results of the first four years, during which major shortfalls occurred in leading sectors of the economy, it appeared highly unlikely that the overall goals of the plan would be met. In a report to the People's Assembly in December 1988, Niko Gjyzari, chairman of the State Planning Commission, failed to disclose plan results for industrial and agricultural production, investments, and exports, indicating they had fallen significantly below official expectations. It is likely that in 1988 industrial production dropped below the record low of 3 percent in 1983, and agricultural production below the record low of 2.2 percent in 1985. Gjyzari said nonfulfillments in the agricultural sector had placed serious burdens on the economy. He sharply criticized the ministries of Agriculture, Industry and Mines, Energy, and Foreign Trade.[11] During 1989, industrial production increased 5.6 percent and agricultural production 9 percent. But despite shortfalls and persistent difficulties, the government continued to stick to highly unrealistic plan targets. Industrial production for 1990 was slated to increase by 8.6 percent and agricultural production by 15 percent.[12]

TABLE 5.3
Allocation of Specialists with Higher Education
(in percentages)

Sector	1970	1980	1985
Education	32.7	34.6	33.4
Industry	14.6	15.1	14.8
Health	12.6	10.8	9.5
Construction	5.2	4.3	3.7
Transportation	1.7	1.2	1.4
Trade	3.1	3.1	3.4
Other	1.3	1.5	2.0

Source: Bardhyl Golemi and Vladimir Misja, *Zhvillimi i arsimit të lartë në Shqipëri* [The Development of Higher Education in Albania] (Tiranë: "8 Nëntori," 1987), p. 182.

THE PERILS OF CENTRAL PLANNING

Alia inherited a command-type economy, with all means of production under state control, agriculture fully collectivized, private enterprise strictly prohibited, and a highly centralized planning and administrative structure. Self-reliance, based on the maximum utilization of internal human, material, and monetary resources and the implementation of a strict savings regime was the main element in the country's development program. In line with a typical Stalinist model of economic development, the APL directed the country's entire economic activity under a single plan.

The economy was plagued by a number of problems: a shortage of skilled workers and managers, low productivity, poor discipline, chronic shortages of basic foodstuffs, and a failing infrastructure. Although the government had devoted great attention to training a labor force, the country still suffered from a shortage of manpower with special skills. In 1985 only 9,130, or 14.8 percent, of the total number of cadres with higher education worked in industry; 2,307, or 3.7 percent, in construction; and 2,115, or 3.4 percent, in the trade sector (Table 5.3). Moreover, less qualified cadres continued to serve in leading positions even in cases where qualified cadres were available. In March 1988 Alia disclosed that "about half the managers of sectors or economic branches have only secondary education." Over 100,000 workers in the agricultural sectors had completed only secondary education, and 5,000 team leaders had only eight years of schooling.[13]

The APL's tight control of the economic decisionmaking process had led to widespread inefficiency and waste. Through huge subsidies, the state had sustained many unprofitable enterprises and kept the prices of food, rent, and other basics absurdly low for decades. By 1986 the state was allocating some 230 million *leks* annually for subsidies of basic goods.[14] Although the government prided itself that prices of some basic commodities had not changed since the 1950s, Albania's decades of stable prices were also years of poverty. Widespread subsidies were dragging down the economy. Untimely investments, construction of grandiose projects in the nonproductive sphere, extravagant use of personnel, and excessive expenditures had become quite common. Machinery and equipment were not properly utilized, particularly in the petroleum industry. According to Minister of Finance Andrea Nako, there were cases when imported machines and equipment were not put to use for years.[15] The press referred to the port of Durrës as "a warehouse," where imported goods stayed idle for months.[16]

Labor productivity reportedly was low, especially in the industrial sector. Influence peddling and petty favoritism, bribery, theft, and worker absenteeism and indifference were said to be widespread.[17] Individuals resorted to family and clan connections to secure better jobs and housing, purchase goods, and obtain permission to travel abroad. Many cadres and workers, including party members, were apathetic toward misappropriations, thefts, and breaches of discipline. In September 1989 Alia disclosed that almost one-third of the working force did not fulfill their norms.[18] Lack of material incentives appeared to be the main cause of the low morale of the work force.

In a meeting with local cadres in Librazhd in September 1987, Alia expressed serious concern about the problem. He disclosed that just in those cases uncovered by the authorities, "thousands of people" were implicated in so-called economic crimes. During 1986 the state incurred "some tens of millions" of *leks* in losses as a result of absenteeism and damage and theft of social property. Such manifestations, Alia said, "hinder the socialist construction of the nation and threaten our social order." He urged that drastic measures be taken against those who stole personal and social property and against saboteurs and criminals.[19] Alia's stern warnings apparently had little effect. Politburo member Simon Stefani, in an article published in May 1988, said continued misappropriations and misuse of common property were causing the economy "great damage."[20] Although officials attributed these "alien manifestations" to remnants of past bourgeois mentality, to many Albanians this explanation no doubt rung hollow.

The authorities also continued to speak out against the growing tendency to engage in private enterprise and black marketeering. Such activities, according to Alia, had reached alarming proportions, especially in cities where residents were turning to private enterpreneurs for such services as house repair, painting, radio and television repair, tailoring, and so on.[21] Although private enterprise played an important role in meeting consumer demands, the government faced an ideological problem as toleration of such activity would lead to unofficial and uncontrollable redistribution of resources. A senior official expressed the view that "private work carried out by particular individuals who fail to carry out properly their tasks in the state enterprises, the use of the private plot for purposes other than that of meeting one's own needs, when the surplus can be sold very well in the state shops, and the working day be invested in common production—all these are alien to socialism."[22]

Officials conceded that one of the reasons for such widespread "alien manifestations" was the inability of the economy to satisfy the population's demands for various goods. It was only after Hoxha's death that the government publicly acknowledged there was not enough meat, fruit, vegetables, and dairy products. Given its emphasis on the development of heavy industry, Hoxha's regime had paid little attention to supplying more and better consumer goods. One of the charges Hoxha had leveled against Mehmet Shehu was that the former prime minister had advocated the development of a consumer society. Shehu reportedly had called for a reallocation of resources away from heavy industry so as to boost the consumer-goods sector.[23] Although about 90 percent of the demand for mass consumer goods was met by domestic production, by 1985 it had become obvious that the situation had deteriorated. Some Albanian analysts were suggesting that grave consequences could result from a continuing failure to address consumers' long-deferred needs.[24]

PROSPECTS FOR ECONOMIC REFORM

Hoxha's highly centralized economic management system, characterized by an absence of initiative and motivation, had stunted economic thinking and appeared uniquely unsuited to tackle the country's growing problems. It seemed doubtful Alia would be able to extricate Albania from its lingering economic difficulties without repudiating some of Hoxha's basic economic principles. Hoxha's death ushered in a political climate more susceptible to calls for economic reform. Only a few months after Alia's accession, a prominent scholar raised the possibility of changes. Writing in the party daily, Hekuran Mara, vice-president of the Academy of Sciences, implied that the new leadership could not rely solely on Hoxha's "thought" as a guide to tackling the country's economic problems. After lauding Hoxha's writings on economic issues, Mara emphasized:

It is, of course, impossible to find the solution to every problem arising in the course of the country's economic development in Comrade Enver's economic thinking. This would be unreasonable and impossible. Comrade Enver's economic thinking generalizes the economic imperative and the objective direction of its development, but the concrete methods, the organizational, technical, administrative and other measures, are the results of subjective activity, constituting what is known as the "corridor for free action" of our people, who are guided by the party's ideology and policy, under conditions of a specific reality, to resolve a specific problem.[25]

During the first five years of his rule, Alia pursued a politically safe economic course, taking approaches that did not differ radically from those advanced in the past but that nevertheless contained some novel aspects. Although not an economist by profession, he displayed an astute awareness of the unsatisfactory state of Albania's economy and its place far behind the economies of the rest of Europe. Soon after he came to power, Alia recognized that food supply was not only an economic but also a serious political problem, and he called for greater emphasis on meeting increasing consumer demands and raising the population's standard of living. In July 1985 he convened a special session of the People's Assembly to deal with supply problems. The Ninth APL Congress gave priority to the development of light and food industries. A series of measures were introduced to encourage the production of various consumer goods and open new production lines. The Ministry of Light and Food Industry was divided into two ministries. Moreover, a State Control Commission was established with the rank of a ministry. It was given widespread executive powers to monitor the execution of the decisions of the Council of Ministers and the implementation of stringent quality controls.[26]

In a major speech at the Third Central Committee Plenum in April 1987, Alia expressed concern about the increasing disparity between production and the population's needs and purchasing power. He insisted that by the end of the 1986–1990 Five-Year Plan, the production of food supplies meet the basic demands of the people in all districts of the country. Alia stressed that "the party should consider the situation in the food market as healthy only when the people can find and buy as much milk and eggs, vegetables, fruit, edible fats, meat, and fish that correspond to their basic needs and their purchasing power."[27] The plenum decided that every district would be responsible to supply its residents with basic foodstuffs.

Alia recognized the importance of private plots in helping alleviate food shortages. In contrast with Hoxha, who had insisted on the reduction and eventual elimination of private plots, Alia urged peasants to raise more livestock and to plant as many vegetables as possible on their land and deliver the surplus to the market. Moreover, he reversed Hoxha's policy of consolidating the collective ownership system. He said transforming agricultural cooperatives into state farms would only lead to increased state subsidies.[28] He stopped short, however, of sanctioning the expansion of private plots and permitting small-scale private enterprise in retail trade and services, which no doubt would have provided a safety valve for economic discontent and would have led to improvements in food supplies, consumer goods, and services. The leadership apparently was concerned that legalizing private business would lead to the emergence of a small class of entrepreneurs, who would earn substantially more than state workers, provoking envy and criticism among the latter. Nevertheless, brigades at the cooperative level were allowed to raise small herds and, after meeting members' demands, to sell surplus produce. To encourage farmers to increase output, the government raised the purchasing prices of agricultural and livestock products.[29]

At the Ninth APL Congress, Alia unveiled facts about mismanagement and the adverse impact of rigid centralization, honed in on the laggards in party and economic organizations, and lashed out at the spread of corruption and indifference. But more importantly, he denounced the excessively centralized economic system and called for a decentralization of the decisionmaking process. Alia sharply criticized "the tendency to centralize even the smaller things, to take away the authority of the lower organs, and to transform the base into a mere executor." He called for greater autonomy for agricultural cooperatives, adding that they "must have greater initiative and authority in determining their own affairs and in finding the more rational ways of increasing their income and production in accordance with their own conditions." He announced a broader reliance on material incentives to encourage production and urged economists to play an expanded role "in order to find the optimal solutions and the most rational ways of using the country's potentials and in order to clarify prospects."[30]

Official pronouncements reflected increasing recognition that the rigid system of central control could no longer keep up with the requirements of a modernizing economy. Although the accent was still on the continuation of Hoxha's policies, the Ninth APL Congress launched a new concept: "New times demand new solutions." In a reversal of traditional development priorities, the Eighth Five-Year Plan emphasized faster growth rates for light and food industries and for agricultural production. In order to deal with the problem of uneven development, the government earmarked extra investments for the less developed hilly and mountainous regions. The leadership instituted a partial decentralization of management, granting more autonomy to lower-level economic units. Because managers had lacked real power and found it difficult to do things strongly opposed by local APL officials, Alia proposed measures to make enterprises more efficient and competitive and to devolve authority to managers, making them less dependent on the center. Moreover, he indicated that he favored giving managers the authority to fire workers and take administrative measures against employees who stole or misappropriated state property, including denying them housing and material benefits.[31] He apparently hoped these steps would unleash initiative in all sections of production and management.

Alia appeared distressed at worker alienation and low labor productivity caused by wage-leveling, overstaffing, and lack of incentives. His proposed solution was to give workers more responsibility and material motivation. A new system of wage incentives, intended to stimulate production by making rewards proportionate to effort, was introduced in some sectors of industry. Workers' wages were linked to the enterprises' profits and their own performances. Alia also raised the possibility of a selective removal or reduction of state subsidies. Acknowledging that some enterprises could not be made profitable, Alia excluded the possibility of permitting them to declare bankruptcy. Unemployment remained an extraordinarily sensitive issue. For years, workers had been told their job security was one of the superior aspects of Albania's communist system.

Some analysts proposed that a price reform be employed to bring supply and demand into balance. Sabah Hilmia, in an article published in July 1986 in the party's theoretical organ, *Rruga e Partisë*, argued that although the APL had pursued "a correct policy of stable prices," such a policy was harming the economy and could not be pursued "forever." He suggested that in setting prices for various industrial and agricultural products, the central planning authorities take into account production costs and the purchasing power of the populace.[32] Another economist, Robert Koli, stressed the need for "a more economic-oriented use of the price lever." He suggested increasing the prices of some food products that did not reflect their real cost value and had been set decades ago under developmental conditions quite different from those of the late 1980s. Koli emphasized:

> Putting quality goods on the market with higher prices and rates of return, and performing quality services at higher tariffs, without affecting calculated and planned consumption, would not only bring improvements in the movement of money, but would also satisfy many demands and wishes expressed continually and over a long period by the working masses for a variety of goods at different prices, according to quality, degree of

processing, packaging, and so forth. At the same time, setting a higher rate of return for these goods and services in comparison with ordinary goods will directly help a better redistribution of incomes among different categories of the population, calling for greater financial commitments on the part of those people with higher incomes.[33]

Although a thoroughgoing reform of both wholesale and retail prices seemed necessary, Alia shied away from a bold price change, fearing that it would lead to social unrest and inflation. Removing or reducing subsidies for rent and other basics would raise living costs. In autumn 1988 speculation about imminent price increases for basic items had apparently caused panic. This prompted Alia to declare that prices for such foodstuffs as sugar, coffee, fats, and meat were "guaranteed" and would not rise.[34]

Bribery, influence peddling, and petty favoritism had become so pervasive that in 1988 Alia resorted to the unprecedented step of replacing all managers or officials in charge of cadre, housing, labor, and residence permit bureaus who had served more than five years in the same positions. To stem the fraying of the moral fabric within party and state organs, the leadership instituted a rule that officials occupying such positions be replaced every five years. Through cadre rotation, the government hoped to ensure good administration.[35]

Measured by the overall performance of the economy, Alia's steps did not seem to have advanced the country much further. The supply situation did not improve significantly and, according to at least one source, the quality of certain goods declined as enterprises continued to concentrate on quantity rather than quality.[36] The State Control Commission came under criticism because of its failure to effect an improvement of the range and quality of goods. The media reported problems in the implementation of party's directives and criticized the inadequate support given to the production of consumer goods and the failure of many enterprises to increase their output. An article in *Rruga e Partisë* in September 1987 complained that there was "a lack of appreciation of the need to develop various branches of the food and light industry, as well as a lack of coordination of duties among the branches of the administration, the retail enterprises, and producers."[37] A Politburo meeting in June 1988 took the trade sector to task for continued inadequacies in meeting growing demands for food supplies.[38] Progress, however, continued to be slow. Alia publicly complained that the planning organs were not giving the necessary support to the development of light and food industries:

The support that the light and food industries require is not a burden on the economy, nor upon heavy industry, and still less upon the priority of heavy industry. It is amazing that in planning, some comrades can really believe that the temporary precedence given to this branch, that demands a few handfuls in investment, can threaten the strategic priority of the heavy industries.[39]

At the end of 1988, the party daily, *Zëri i Popullit*, reported delays in starting construction work in seventeen plans in the food industry. The paper said that central planning authorities and local officials were holding back investments for light industrial and food-producing factories for the sake of giving priority to heavy industry.[40]

Alia expressed dismay that some enterprises could continue to produce the same shoddy goods for decades, although the needs and tastes of the consumers had risen drastically.[41] The problem was further complicated by the state's inability to match the population's increasing purchasing power with goods and services. One analyst warned of dire political consequences if the situation was not remedied soon.[42] The problem of low quality was not restricted just to the consumer sector. According to an editorial in *Zëri i Popullit*, in 1987 alone enterprises under the Ministry of Transportation had sent back to the engineering industry 42,000 spare parts because of poor quality.[43]

The Albanian leader continued to voice concern at the dismal performance of the agricultural sector. At the Seventh Central Committee Plenum held in February 1989, Alia said that changes in production relations and outdated regulations and norms had become indispensable. In what may have been his most important statement to date on the need for reform, he insisted that "there was nothing wrong" with instituting changes in order to deal with new problems and provide new impulses to development. He added:

> It is essential to bear in mind, first, that whenever changes become necessary to further promote development there must be no hesitation in making relevant suggestions. Timidity and slowness only increase difficulties and hinder development; secondly, we must never think that the measures in the field of economic relations are given once and for all times and that, when adopted, they have only positive effects, that they are ideal and without potential shortcomings. Such measures do not exist.

He warned that the continuation of the poor state of affairs in agriculture "would be accompanied by harmful political effects."[44] The Seventh Central Committee Plenum emphasized the use of material incentives to reward good workers and boost production. It also approved measures to give cooperatives greater autonomy. The cooperatives were permitted to distribute the value of above-plan production to their members, after costs and a reasonable sum for accumulation had been deducted. In addition, the cooperatives would sell their surplus production, as well as products gathered from personal plots and from brigade members, directly on the market. Retail prices of these products would reflect production costs and supply and demand and would be higher than those for the same products sold by state farms.[45] Alia said that the new measures would lead to income differentiation but noted that egalitarianism, one of the most important aspects of Hoxha's economic policy, "is always to the benefit of those who seek from society more than they are prepared to give it. . . . If we want development, we must support and stimulate those who are more advanced and who, on the basis of the present system of remuneration, are dealt with on an equal basis with those who exert themselves less."[46]

Many party and government officials were not up to the new way of doing things that Alia required of them. To some extent, the bureaucracy was successful in undercutting the new policies. Conservatives were not ready to abandon the command-administrative habits or the privileges to which they had become accustomed. They viewed labor unrest in Poland and in neighboring Yugoslavia as case studies of the dangers that lurk in decentralization and the weakening of party's monopoly. Hard-liners feared that attempts to liberalize the system of economic management would lead inexorably to demands for political reform. They considered as "unsocialist" and "bourgeois" any attempt to reduce state control and introduce a new wage and price system.

That Alia faced opposition in his efforts to reinvigorate the economy became evident at the Ninth APL Congress. He lashed out at hard-liners who apparently were against the implementation of economic changes, advocating instead reliance on more orthodox socialist policies:

> Sectarianism is harmful as a concept, since it holds fast to things gone by; it does not see changes and transformations that are taking place, changes in material conditions and in social conditions, especially in the spiritual life of society. Unable to understand the dialectic of life, it falls into conservatism and dogmatism.[47]

Subsequently, Alia disclosed that there was particular resistance, based on ideological grounds, to the policy of having brigades at the cooperative level raise small herds. The most obstinate opposition had been offered by recalcitrant cadres, who warned that such a policy would lead to the reintroduction of private property.[48] Alia suggested that hard-liners should be more concerned with meeting the population's demands, adding that the private market flourishes when the state is unable to meet such demands.[49] At a Politburo meeting in April 1987, Alia again complained about bureaucratic hindrance to the implementation of new policies. He said it had taken "several" meetings of the Central Committee before the initiative could be taken to have brigades raise herds.[50]

Politburo member Foto Çami, who emerged as the leadership's point man in advocating economic reforms, lamented that calls for changes were coming only from the top. In a speech at the Academy of Sciences in March 1987, he asserted that recent economic policies had encountered opposition at middle levels of the bureaucracy. Although presumably addressing a friendly audience, Çami, a prominent member of the intelligentsia, apparently felt the need to justify changes introduced after the Ninth APL Congress. He said socialism in Albania would in no way suffer as a result of the establishment of small herds at the brigade level, changes in wages and prices, and the granting of greater autonomy to agricultural cooperatives.[51]

The critical tone of Alia's pronouncements was an indication of the seriousness with which he viewed the country's economic problems and the need for change. In a speech at the party *aktiv* (activists) in Tiranë in March 1987, he drew a distinction between what he described as "primary" tenets of the system, which "must be preserved and developed," and "secondary" ones, which must undergo constant "change and refinement."[52] Echoing Alia's pronouncements, Premier Adil Çarçani said there was a need for a new approach, insisting that party cadres should "not remain slaves of practices and methods which have been overtaken by time."[53]

Much of the criticism permeating official statements and media reports on economic affairs continued to be directed at overcentralization, management problems, low labor productivity, and the inability to spur initiative in all sections of production and management. Çami displayed a novel style, going further than both Alia and Çarçani in stressing the need for "new solutions." In what appeared to be a radical proposal in Albania's context, Çami asserted that as long as the country's freedom and independence were protected and the social order preserved, "other things can and must be changed when necessary, suffice that they do not affect the foundations of our socialist system, but serve them."[54] In a major address in October 1987, Çami said Marxism-Leninism provided only basic guidelines and that "it would be wrong and naive to demand from it schemes and ready-made recipes for all the specific issues which arise in the course of social practice." Everything must be subjected to the test of practice, he said, adding that matters that "are not questions of principle and do not run counter to the foundations of our socialist system, can and must be changed when the time demands it, and when it is made necessary by the needs of the development of the country, and the interests of the homeland and of socialism." Reflecting the leadership's growing impatience with economists, theoreticians, and ideologues who had lagged behind practical developments instead of taking the lead in formulating ideas that would have made a useful impact, he reproached officials and cadres who waited for instructions and orders from above. Çami added:

> There is a dominant way of thinking among many cadres that I would call metaphysical. They see themselves more as channels and simple performers of instructions and decisions. They have a harmful tendency only to be led from above, wanting the leadership to say or demand everything, hesitating or not exerting their brains to raise problems and offer suggestions for creative solutions, changes, and refinements that must be introduced into our past practice, and so on. Such a spirit and attitude leads to dogmatism and conservatism, to becoming a slave to habits and old forms and methods that are unsuitable or which have been superseded by time. As the 9th APL Congress pointed out, it even leads to the creation of a social type who is frightened of everything that is new, of all kinds of change, and who becomes an obstacle to further progress.[55]

Changing economic thought and practice appeared to be an incredibly difficult task. Despite the leadership's calls for a greater role for experts, most economists were reluctant to speak out for fear they might commit ideological or political errors. The APL's tendency in the past had been to blame individuals for economic failures. The imprisonment and execution of senior economic officials in the mid-1970s and their becoming scapegoats for economic failures had apparently remained seared in the collective memory of economic experts. Alia tried to convince economists to air their views freely, insisting that their input "was now needed more than ever before."[56] Nevertheless, it was not clear where the leadership would draw the line and what suggestions it would countenance from experts.

CONCLUSION

Although the post-Hoxha leadership seemed to have created a favorable climate for economic change, Alia did not radically modify his predecessors' policies. The introduction of radical reform, including full decentralization, disentangling the party from the management of the economy, and repudiating the principle of self-reliance, would suggest that past policies of the Albanian Communist government, which still retained its Stalinist character, had all along been fatally flawed. Although official pronouncements reflected strong rhetoric on the need for change, the leadership assumed a cautious approach. By the end of the 1980s, Alia had not yet offered a blueprint nor had he created an institutionalized base for fundamental reform. If the drive for economic revival produced isolated success stories, it did not raise the general standard of living. The supplies and quality of food, housing, and basic consumer goods did not improve noticeably, leading to heightened popular disenchantment with the grim economic reality. The economy was still managed in a cumbersome way, with a perverse system of economic incentives and planning. Party organs continued to duplicate the functions of state organs and in most cases still had the last word. There was little likelihood the APL would soon decide to concentrate on its proper role of overall guidance and get out of the day-to-day operations that were the business of state organs.

In order to revitalize the economy, Alia would probably have to undo four decades of Stalinist central planning and overcome tremendous resistance based as much on Hoxha's legacy as on the country's conservative culture. The regime, however, feared that economic liberalization and encouragement of individual initiative would mean political liberalization and uncontrollable consequences, threatening the party's hold on power. Implementing meaningful reforms involved trading current job security for greater future opportunity and posed, at least in the short run, serious political risks. Shutting down outmoded industries and unprofitable enterprises was politically unacceptable and would lead to unemployment and bankruptcy. Removing or reducing subsidies and increasing prices would trigger inflation, consumer panic, and a significant cost of living increase. Moreover, strong conservative elements within the party and the government opposed measures that threatened to loosen the party's ideological controls.

With such strong impediments to change, radical reform seemed highly unlikely. But the alternative was analogously unacceptable to Alia. Unless measures were taken to redress some of the most damaging aspects of Hoxha's economic policy, there would be a high probability that in the 1990s Albania would be confronted with social upheavals. At the minimum, the failure to find a way out of the economic impasse, would likely cause Albania to sink to the developmental level of poor Third World countries. Alia opted for partial reforms and tried to tackle economic problems without tampering with the fundamental features of the system. Although the long-term success of his policies remained highly ambivalent, he started a slow process of economic change and, perhaps more encouraging, held out the promise that more significant reforms were forthcoming. But no economic reforms are likely to succeed if they are not backed up with similar political changes, a more responsible use of power by the governing elite, and an institutionalization of cooperative relations with the outside world.

6

Foreign Policy

Albania is a small state, with limited human and material resources, whose primary foreign policy objective historically has been the preservation of its independence and territorial integrity. Its post–World War II foreign policy was characterized by dramatic shifts. Enver Hoxha relied on alliances with communist states that provided substantial foreign aid for Albania's economic development and supported his regime's objectives of retaining power, attaining economic self-sufficiency in as many sectors as possible, and creating a new, "Marxist-Leninist" value system. Over a period of thirty-three years, Albania progressed from a Yugoslav subsatellite (1945–1948), to a Soviet satellite (1948–1961), to a Chinese ally (1961–1978) and finally asserted its decisionmaking autonomy and broke out of a dependent relationship, becoming perhaps Europe's most independent country.

The scope, nature, and level of Albania's external interaction differed substantially from those of its neighbors. Of all the Eastern European countries, Albania had been least involved in international politics in the post–World War II era. After its break with the Soviet Union in 1961, the Albanian Party of Labor severed its contacts with the international Communist movement (with the exception of the Chinese Communist Party and the insignificant splinter Marxist-Leninist parties that had emerged in the wake of the Sino-Soviet rift) and embarked on a self-imposed isolationist policy. With the disruption of ideological and economic ties with China in 1978, Albania rejected future alliances, insisting on an independent foreign policy.

Several interrelated factors determined Albania's foreign policy, the most important ones being nationalism, economic necessity, ideology, and the APL leadership's concern for domestic stability. Nationalism no doubt was the most important determinant. Historically, the fate of Albania had been one of domination and threat by its more powerful neighbors—Greece, Italy, and Yugoslavia. The nationalist aspirations of the Albanian nation remained unfulfilled. The country's partition in 1912

85

and the loss of Kosovë and other compact, Albanian-inhabited territories had psychologically scarred the Albanian nation, fostering xenophobia and a siege mentality on the part of many of its citizens and leaders. The Albanians attributed their inability to achieve national union to the hostile policies of their neighbors, supported by the major powers. Traditional fears of Albanian dismemberment and foreign domination and subjugation persisted. This paranoid attitude toward the outside world was further reinforced by Hoxha's obsession with internal and external enemies and by official propaganda that maintained Albania had suffered humiliation, partition, and foreign domination because of its political, economic, and military weakness. Many Albanians in the PSRA, Kosovë, and abroad had come to perceive the outside world as essentially hostile or indifferent to their national goals and welfare.

The APL leadership had given paramount importance to the restoration and preservation of the country's political independence. As Julian Birch noted, Hoxha displayed "a marked reluctance to make Albania merely the puppet of those whose protection and aid was sought; while at the same time his would-be guardians have shown a similar determination to undermine the regime or at least to get some political interest in return for their investment."[1] The nation's political stance had determined its foreign economic policy. Between 1945 and 1978, Albania received substantial foreign assistance from its communist allies. But economic dependence made Albania vulnerable to pressures, threats, and interferences in its domestic affairs.

Albania's negative experience with its aid donors had given rise to a perception that reliance on foreign assistance leads to economic dependence, which in turn compromises the country's political independence. Following the break with China, Albania embarked on a costly policy of self-reliance. It was probably the only state in the world that had a constitutional provision prohibiting its government from seeking foreign aid and credits, granting concessions to foreign corporations, or forming joint companies. Hoxha sought to create the illusion that Albania had no alternative to an inward orientation because, as the only truly "socialist" country in the world, it was surrounded and blockaded by "imperialist" and "revisionist" states allegedly bent on its destruction.

Hoxha had adopted a dogmatic interpretation of Marxism-Leninism and followed a policy rhetorically reminiscent of the cold war era. The most salient ideological aspects of his foreign policy were the division of the world into two opposing systems—socialism and capitalism—and the two-front struggle against U.S. "imperialism" and Soviet "social-imperialism." These principles were also embodied in the constitution. The rigid classification of various countries according to their socioeconomic order did not prevent Albania, even during Hoxha's era, from developing cordial relations with many Western and Third World countries. But the "dual-adversary" strategy, which held that the two superpowers were equally "dangerous" and "aggressive," had prevented Tiranë from reaching an accommodation with Washington and Moscow. Albania continued to view the two superpowers as cooperating and competing, simultaneously, in dividing the world into spheres of influence. It refused to participate in negotiations for the Conference on Security and Cooperation in Europe (CSCE) and was the only European country that did not sign the Helsinki Final Act in 1975 and did not participate in CSCE follow-up meetings. Its major objection was that the CSCE was sponsored by the United States and the Soviet Union, precisely the powers that in Tiranë's view threatened "peace and security" in Europe. Pursuing an even-handed approach toward the two superpowers, the Albanian government expressed opposition to virtually every U.S. and Soviet international initiative. Before Hoxha's death, Albania also refused to take part in regional multilateral cooperation, arguing that such efforts were futile because of the influence of the superpowers.

Albania's foreign policy had also been affected by personal power considerations of the ruling elite. The primary objective of the APL had been to maintain its power and control over the country. Hoxha ruled the country with an iron hand, and any outside power that actually or potentially undermined his regime was cast in the role of an enemy. Tiranë's inherent mistrust of Belgrade, Washington, and Moscow may in part be attributed to reported Yugoslav, U.S., and Soviet attempts to overthrow or undermine Hoxha's regime in the 1950s and the 1960s. Moreover, Hoxha viewed the establishment of uncontrolled or significant contacts with other countries as inimical to the APL's ideological interests and internally destabilizing, as they could encourage domestic forces to advocate long-overdue systemic reforms. In fact, he used the myth of Albania's being constantly threatened by external and internal enemies in order to justify the implementation of radical internal policies.

ALBANIA'S OPENING UP IN THE EARLY 1980s

In the wake of the break with China, Albania found itself in the unenviable position of being Europe's most isolated nation. Foreign policy had apparently become a divisive issue in leadership debates, with Premier Mehmet Shehu reportedly advocating a greater opening up toward the West[2] and Hoxha insisting on a policy of "going-it-alone." Self-imposed isolation produced immediate adverse economic consequences. As a result, Hoxha was forced to sanction a cautious process of strengthening bilateral relations with neighboring countries, particularly Yugoslavia. Although Albanian media attacks against its neighbor had increased during the last phase of the Tiranë-Beijing alliance, when Yugoslav and Chinese leaders exchanged visits, both Albania and Yugoslavia came to understand that they shared a common enemy, the Soviet Union. In addition, Yugoslavia, faced with the resurgence of nationalism and growing unrest among ethnic Albanians and concerned about Tiranë's post-Hoxha foreign policy orientation, was eager to develop an elaborate and interdependent relationship with its neighbor. Following the Soviet invasion of Afghanistan in 1979, Albania repeated its offer, first made after the Warsaw Pact invasion of Czechoslovakia in 1968, to come to Yugoslavia's assistance in the event of an external attack. The two countries also signed an agreement on a railroad linkage between Shkodër and Titograd. Bilateral cultural contacts increased significantly, and there was a rapid expansion of economic cooperation. By 1980 Yugoslavia had replaced China as Albania's main trading partner, accounting for close to 20 percent of Albania's total foreign trade.

The expansion of relations with other neighbors was less striking than that with Yugoslavia but nonetheless significant. Moreover, the cut in Chinese foreign aid and Beijing's refusal to trade with Tiranë caused a major reorientation in Albania's foreign trade. Short of hard currency and refusing to seek foreign credits and loans, Albania was forced to sharply reduce its imports. In search of new markets, it turned to its immediate neighbors as well as to Western Europe and to the members of the CMEA but refused to engage in trade exchanges with the Soviet Union.

By the early 1980s, growing economic difficulties and tensions with Yugoslavia following the March–April 1981 demonstrations by ethnic Albanians in Kosovë prompted Albania to embrace a more pragmatic foreign policy, especially toward Greece, Turkey, and Western Europe. As had often been the case in past realignments, the major foreign policy determinants were concern with security implications and long-term Yugoslav intentions toward Albania. The rapid deterioration of relations with Belgrade after the Yugoslav military suppression of Albanian demonstrations in Kosovë underscored the risks of Albania's isolation.

As Hoxha's era approached its end and Ramiz Alia emerged as heir apparent, some interesting shifts could be discerned in Albania's foreign policy. The nation took gradual steps to emerge from its self-imposed isolation and limit the adverse economic and political consequences of the conflict with Yugoslavia. During a tour in June 1983 of the northern district of Tropojë, Alia indicated that his country had embarked on a more pragmatic foreign policy. Rejecting Yugoslav allegations that Tiranë was responsible for the unrest in Kosovë, Alia acknowledged a diplomatic shift away from Yugoslavia and toward Italy, Greece, and Turkey. He said Albania favored the normalization and expansion of ties with all other countries with the exception of the superpowers.[3] In a major policy address in November 1984, Alia reaffirmed interest in expanding relations with other countries, especially those in Western Europe, adding that "Albania is a European country and as such it is vitally interested in what is occurring on that continent."[4]

The policy of opening up was reflected in a substantial increase in diplomatic activity, the signing of numerous agreements on economic and cultural cooperation, the exchange of ministerial-level delegations, and greater participation in international trade fairs. Against the background of mounting tensions with Yugoslavia, Albania took diplomatic initiatives to strengthen relations with Italy and Greece. In 1983 Albania and Italy signed an agreement on establishing a maritime line linking the ports of Durrës and Trieste. The two countries also signed a long-term trade agreement. In return for raw materials, Italy agreed to supply Albania with industrial technology.[5] Albania also sought technical assistance in locating and exploiting oil deposits on its Adriatic coast and held talks with the Italian firm AGIP.[6] In an interview during a visit to Rome in December 1984, Deputy Foreign Minister Sokrat Plaka said his country was "seeking partners in the West and . . . looking to Italy in particular in view of the social and cultural ties between the two countries."[7]

Meanwhile, Tiranë also improved relations with Athens. In December 1984 Albania and Greece signed a long-term economic accord as well as agreements on road transportation, cultural exchanges, scientific and technological cooperation, telecommunications, and postal services. A month later, the Kakavija border road in the Gjirokastër district was reopened—the first road link between the two countries since 1945. Cultural and trade exchanges increased substantially, and the Albanians agreed to establish a department for Greek Studies at the Tiranë Pedagogical Institute.

Albania's expansion of interactions with Greece and Italy as well as with Turkey, Austria, and some other Western European countries caused consternation and mistrust in Belgrade. Obviously, the Yugoslavs preferred to see Albania remain isolated. The Albanians, on the other hand, recognizing Yugoslavia's strategic importance and prestige in the international arena, apparently feared that Western European countries would allow Belgrade to dictate policies toward Tiranë. Such a concern was expressed by Alia, who declared that the outside world "cannot possibly see Albania and its policy through the spectacles of Belgrade."[8]

Albania's diplomatic initiatives were accompanied by a notable change in the tone of propaganda and a playing down of ideology in foreign policy pronouncements. The APL attenuated its relations with splinter Marxist-Leninist parties and virtually ceased its calls for a "world proletarian revolution." Albania sought instead to stabilize bilateral relations with various countries, irrespective of their social systems, but continued to offer rhetorical support to a large number of revolutionary movements in Latin America, Africa, the Middle East, and Asia. In the United Nations, it still cast its lot with the Third World, consistently voting against the West on a wide range of issues. On some issues, such as Kampuchea, Albania's position coincided with that of the Soviet Union and its allies. On the other hand, Albania sharply denounced Soviet actions in Afghanistan and its disruptive efforts in many parts of the world.

ALIA: FOREIGN POLICY PRAGMATISM

Ramiz Alia inherited a relatively auspicious external environment, most Western and Eastern European countries, including the two superpowers, having adopted a benevolent attitude toward Albania. Although adherence to a rigid Stalinist ideology had made Albania's one of the most politically repressive regimes in Eastern Europe, it found other governments quite receptive to its initiatives for improvement of relations. Since the early 1960s, Western European countries had become sensitive to the benefits of Albania's independence from the Soviet bloc. Tiranë's break with Moscow had contributed significantly to Western interests in the Balkans. As in the case of Yugoslavia, Western European capitals played down the question of human rights violations in their overtures to Albania, giving precedence to that country's strategic importance. Similarly, the United States, beginning in 1973, expressed willingness to resume ties with Albania. It was in the United States' interest that Albania continue to pursue an independent foreign policy and not reestablish close—especially military—ties with the Soviet Union. A revival of the Albanian-Soviet alliance would give the USSR military access to the Adriatic, increase potential Soviet pressure on Yugoslavia and Greece, and heighten the threat to NATO's southern flank. An independent, nonaligned Albania was thus important for Western policy in the volatile Balkans. After Hoxha's death, senior U.S. officials reiterated that "should Albania indicate an interest in resuming relations with us, we would be prepared to respond."[9]

Soviet bloc policy toward Albania also had undergone important changes. In the early 1960s the Soviets, distressed that Albania had taken the Chinese side in the Sino-Soviet conflict, cut all relations with Tiranë, resorted to political and economic pressures, attempted to incite popular dissatisfaction against Hoxha's regime, and excluded Albania from the Warsaw Pact and CMEA. As Albania proceeded with its own model of communist development, Hoxha in the mid- and late 1960s took measures to eradicate signs of Soviet influence and legacy from all parts of Albanian society. After Khrushchev's downfall in 1964, Moscow expressed willingness to normalize relations. Tiranë, however, insisted that the Soviets first apologize publicly for their decision to break diplomatic relations in 1961, a condition the Kremlin refused to accept. During the last phase, and after the disintegration of the Albanian-Chinese alliance, the Soviets adopted a friendly attitude toward Albania. They hoped to reestablish diplomatic relations and prevent Albania from joining Western political and military organizations.

The Soviets were especially persistent in their efforts to woo Albania back into their fold, offering badly needed loans and credits, experts, and modern technology. Realizing that, as in the case of Yugoslavia in the late 1940s, pressure on Albania had been counterproductive, the Soviets reversed their policy of trying to isolate the country and attempting to incite popular dissatisfaction against the regime. Instead, Moscow invited Tiranë to take its place in the Warsaw Pact and CMEA, and praised Albania for "successfully building socialism." In 1986 the Soviet party organ, *Pravda*, blamed Khrushchev's "subjectivism and voluntarism" for the Tiranë-Moscow break.[10] Soviet bloc media continued to emphasize the economic and political benefits of Albania's return to the fold. The Soviets were not discouraged by Albania's negative response to their offers.

With Hoxha's death in April 1985, a reassessment of Albania's foreign policy had become inevitable. Adverse economic consequences, caused primarily by a long period of isolation and reflected most dramatically in the unfulfillment of economic targets and chronic shortages, made it imperative that Albania interact more with the outside world. While still abiding by the principle of barter trade, Alia rejected suggestions by officials of the Foreign Trade Ministry that imports be drastically reduced. Such a policy, he insisted, would seriously hinder the country's long-term economic development.[11] He appeared intent on introducing modern technology into all fields. Backward technology had hampered the development of the industrial sector, and Albania was particularly in need of updating equipment in the mining and oil industries in order to exploit fully its reserves of chrome, nickel, copper, natural gas, iron, coal, lignite, and oil. In a speech at a conference on technological innovation in Shkodër in September 1985, Alia asserted that "we are still far away from what we intend to achieve." He called for structural improvements in production, adding that it was an "absolute necessity" to boldly introduce advanced methods and technology in design and production.[12]

The Albanians realized that the technological modernization of the economy could not be achieved without greater economic interaction with the outside world. Sofokli Lazri, a member of the party's Central Committee and director of the Foreign Affairs Institute, disclosed at the Ninth APL Congress in November 1986, that Albania would significantly expand trade exchanges with other countries, importing factories, equipment, and various kinds of modern technology.[13] The Albanian government evidently hoped that the introduction of more advanced technology would alleviate the country's economic difficulties. Limited foreign reserves and constitutional bans on foreign loans and credits, however, continued to restrict the country's technology imports. Moreover, with the shortage of qualified experts, Albania experienced difficulty absorbing and fully utilizing new technology.

Albania's opening up was undoubtedly motivated by economic necessity, but political considerations were also important. Hoxha's isolationist policy, which had deprived the country of the political and economic advantages of greater interaction with the outside world, was not viable in the long run. Moreover, with the exasperation of the ethnic conflict in Kosovë, Yugoslavia had resorted to economic, military, and political pressures on Albania. A major objective of Albanian diplomacy became the prevention of the establishment of an anti-Albanian Balkan coalition directed by Belgrade. This required the stabilization and strengthening of relations with other countries, particularly neighboring Greece, Italy, and Bulgaria.

One of the main characteristics of Hoxha's foreign policy had been the view that Albania's immediate neighbors—individually or collectively—represented the main sources of external threat. This perception accounted for Albania's refusal to join its neighbors in attempts at multilateral cooperation. Hoxha had warned repeatedly that the superpowers represented the primary danger to stability in the Balkans and had called on Greece and Turkey, and Bulgaria and Romania to withdraw from NATO and the Warsaw Pact respectively. He also had urged Yugoslavia to deny Soviet and U.S. navies access to its ports and facilities.

Soon after Alia's accession to power, significant changes became evident in Albanian perceptions about international politics, signaling that the post-Hoxha leadership would inject a new flexibility into foreign policy and do away with the most damaging self-imposed constraints that had limited the country's options. The Albanians moved away from some of the old stereotypes propagated by the official media for decades; the outside world was no longer portrayed in black-and-white terms. Albania now appeared willing to take advantage of disagreements among its immediate neighbors, pursuing a differentiation policy toward them. Neighboring countries were no longer characterized collectively as sources of external threat, although Yugoslavia continued to be cast in the role of a country essentially hostile to Albania's national goals and objectives.

Senior officials went out of their way to deny that Hoxha had pursued an isolationist policy or that Albania was "isolated."[14] Deputy Foreign Minister Muhamet Kapllani, in an article published in the party's theoretical journal soon after Hoxha's death, asserted that the Albanian party and state were "in favor of an active as opposed to a passive policy."[15] In July 1985 the government published a posthumous work by Hoxha, the main thesis of which supported Albania's efforts to emerge from isolation. In that book, Hoxha asserted that whenever it had been in Albania's national interest to "open up" to the outside world, it had done so, and that it would do the same in the future.[16] Politburo member Foto Çami stressed that Albania "has never been, and is not in favor of a policy of self-enclosure." He argued that the expansion of relations was

> in the country's interest, because it reinforces its international position, and creates more favorable and tranquil conditions for socialist construction, giving opportunities for the trading, cultural, technical, and scientific exchanges which are so necessary for the country's development. But there can be no doubt that expanding these relations also creates problems, especially in increasing the pressure of alien ideology upon our people. Yet we can and must confront this with our ever more professional and persuasive work, putting the great interests of the country, at which our foreign policy aims, before everything else.[17]

In public statements, Alia indicated that his foreign policy would focus less on the regime's Marxist-Leninist ideology and more on political and economic realities confronting Albania. In a speech at the Fourth Plenum of the Central Committee in July 1987, he said, "The tactics followed in the field of our international relations change, since problems change and evolve in the ebb and flow of revolutionary national liberation movements, new issues arise requiring fresh consideration, and so on."[18] On the occasion of the seventy-fifth anniversary of Albania's independence, Alia said, "We do not intend to stand aside from the rest of the world, or to live in isolation. We do not hesitate to cooperate with others and we do not fear their power and wealth. On the contrary, we seek such cooperation since we consider it a factor that will contribute to our internal development."[19]

RELATIONS WITH NEIGHBORS

Foreign policy pragmatism in the post-Hoxha era was perhaps best dramatized by Albania's participation in the Balkan Foreign Ministers

Conference, held in Belgrade in February 1988. Initially, Tiranë's reaction to the Yugoslav foreign minister's proposal was lukewarm. In July 1987 Alia, although insisting that Albania had no "prejudices" about the Yugoslav proposal, termed it an attempt by the post-Tito leadership to recover its "lost authority."[20] The first signs that Albania might accept the Yugoslav invitation emerged in September 1987 when Foreign Minister Reis Malile asserted, in an address to the UN General Assembly, that Albania "in principle" favored "bilateral and multilateral meetings and talks."[21] He met with his Yugoslav counterpart, and shortly afterwards Albania announced that it had accepted the Yugoslav proposal. Greece, which by this time had developed close ties with Albania, played an important role in convincing Albania to attend the conference.[22]

At the meeting, Malile maintained what a Yugoslav official called "a constructive and conciliatory" stand.[23] He said that Albania "is for the independent development and stability of each Balkan country. We are aware that destabilization of any of our countries is to the detriment of each of us and of peace and security in general." He called for the reactivation of Balkan committees on trade, transportation, and other issues. "Not only do we not hesitate to cooperate with others, but, on the contrary, we want this cooperation and consider it a factor which contributes to our internal development too," he said. Without mentioning the thorny issue of Kosovë, Malile declared that minorities

> should be turned into a factor of cohesion and stability within the country and a bridge for relations of cooperation with the neighboring countries. Our times are not those of colonizations, of the oppression of the minorities and the suppression of their rights which are recognized by international law and the Charter of the United Nations.[24]

In January 1989 Tiranë hosted the meeting of Balkan deputy foreign ministers—the first regional multilateral meeting held in Tiranë in the post-1945 period. Albania also agreed to host the 1990 Balkan Foreign Ministers Conference.[25]

Throughout the 1960s and 1970s, Tiranë had boycotted all regional attempts at multilateral cooperation. Albania's participation in the Belgrade conference represented an important departure from Hoxha's policies. It marked the beginning of a new phase in Albania's foreign policy and the clearest indication of Alia's determination to return his country to the mainstream of international politics. With the participation in Balkan regional meetings, Alia for all practical purposes ended his country's isolation.

Yugoslavia

Tiranë-Belgrade relations had traditionally been problematic because of the presence of the approximately 2.5 million ethnic Albanians in Yugoslavia, most of whom lived in the province of Kosovë, contiguous to Albania.[26] After the Soviet invasion of Czechoslovakia, Albania had subordinated its ethnic ties with the Albanians in Kosovë to its overall political, security, and economic interests vis-à-vis Yugoslavia. After years of mistrust and minimum contact, the two countries came to share the perception that their independence was threatened by a common enemy—the Soviet Union. There was mutual recognition of increasing interdependence and interest in opposing the presence of the great powers in the Balkans. The 1970s had witnessed a new era in Albanian-Yugoslav relations, characterized by an unprecedented cooperation, particularly in economic and cultural fields.

Nationalist disturbances in Kosovë in 1981, however, led to a rapid and dramatic deterioration of relations between Albania and Yugoslavia. Mutual recriminations followed events in Kosovë, with Albania supporting Kosovar demands that their province be given the status of a republic, and Yugoslavia accusing Albania of intervening in its internal affairs. As a result, bilateral cultural cooperation was halted and political and economic contacts severely curtailed.

Alia's government continued to express concern about the fate of Albanians in Yugoslavia. Because the Kosovars accounted for almost half of the Albanian nation, Tiranë could not remain neutral in the Kosovë conflict. But Albania had nothing to gain from disturbances in Kosovë and the destabilization of Yugoslavia. Despite long-standing political and ideological differences with Yugoslavia, the Albanian government expressed support for its neighbor's independence and national integrity. Officials in Tiranë repeatedly stated that Albania had no territorial claims on Yugoslavia. In his keynote address to the Ninth APL Congress in November 1986, Alia said, "We do not want the situation in Kosovë to grow worse. In no instance and in no way have we sought or do we seek to destabilize Yugoslavia. It is not in the interest of the peoples in the Balkans, nor in our interest, that [Yugoslavia] should be turned into an arena of quarrels and dissent, a situation which could facilitate the interference of foreign powers."[27]

Despite his concern about the plight of ethnic Albanians, Alia recognized the necessity of finding a modus vivendi with Yugoslavia and sought to move from confrontation to reconciliation. Immediately after Alia's accession to power, Albania's anti-Yugoslav diatribes declined. Significantly, neither in his report to the Ninth APL Congress nor in other public statements did Alia endorse Kosovar demands for a republic.

In a speech in January 1987, the Albanian leader said, "The demand for a Kosovë republic was not raised in Albania, but in Kosovë as a demand for the same rights, work and equality as enjoyed by all the other peoples in Yugoslavia."[28]

Albania's conciliatory tone was perhaps best demonstrated at the Balkan Foreign Ministers Conference. In an unprecedented declaration, Malile said the status of Kosovë was essentially a Yugoslav internal issue:

> Certainly, the stand toward minorities and their treatment is an internal question of each country, a field of its complete sovereignty, which is treated in compliance with the state system and the laws of each country. The People's Socialist Republic of Albania has never raised the question that the issue of the minorities should be solved by changing borders and interfering in the internal affairs of one another. But we think that this does not rule out the legitimate interest of neighbors in their minorities, especially in those cases when this interest is based on the will and the sincere desire to contribute to the strengthening of the good neighborliness and friendship among peoples, to the general security in the Balkans.[29]

The Belgrade conference contributed to an improvement in the political atmosphere. It also provided fresh impulses for the expansion of cultural and economic cooperation. In the wake of the unrest in Kosovë in 1981, Belgrade had halted all cultural exchanges with Tiranë. The prominent Kosovar scholar Rexhep Qosja had described the lack of cultural contact between the two neighboring countries as "truly an extraordinary anachronism, not only for Europe, but for the world." He told the Ljubljana newspaper *Delo* that "one can travel, for example, from Belgrade or Tiranë to Tokyo, São Paulo, or any other city in the world in a day. People have even gone to the moon and are still planning to travel to other planets, but one still cannot go from Prishtinë to Tiranë or from Tiranë to Prishtinë."[30] Throughout the 1980s, trade between the two countries had stagnated, primarily because of political tensions in their relations but also because of Albania's inability, due to several years of serious drought, to supply Yugoslavia with the contracted quantity of electricity—its most important export item. In 1982 bilateral trade had reached a record of $147.9 million, but in 1987 it amounted to $63 million, and in 1988 it dropped to $50 million.

On the eve of the Balkan Foreign Ministers Conference and after years of deadlock, Tiranë and Belgrade concluded an agreement on cultural exchanges. This was followed with the signing of an agreement on border trade and the linkup of an electric power station in Prizren, Kosovë, with the hydroelectric power plant in Fierzë, northern Albania.

Moreover, amid reports of growing numbers of Yugoslavs visiting Albania, the Ljubljana tourist agency Kompas received a license to advertise trips to Albania's Adriatic coast.[31] For Albania, the signing of the border trade agreement was particularly important. With the conclusion of this and a similar agreement with Greece, Albania hoped to alleviate chronic shortages of consumer goods, while at the same time minimizing foreign exchange expenditures and transportation costs. And during bilateral discussions in Tiranë in January 1989, the Albanian government reportedly proposed an expansion of economic cooperation, including the proposal that the Yugoslavs build and equip a mine in the PSRA in return for deliveries of ore.[32]

Despite these positive developments, Albanian-Yugoslav relations remained tense, particularly following the imposition of special security measures and the dispatch of federal army and militia units in Kosovë in February and March 1989 and subsequent violent clashes between security forces and Albanian demonstrators. A statement by the official news agency, ATA, denounced what it termed "the chauvinist policy" being pursued against ethnic Albanians. It called on the Yugoslav and world public opinion to defend Kosovars' human and national rights:

> It is not up only to the Albanian people to defend the legitimate rights of Albanians in Yugoslavia. This should be done by all who really respect Yugoslavia and wish its stability and well-being. . . . The national and democratic rights of Yugoslavia's peoples and nations, including the Albanians, should also be defended by those who desire that the long-suffering Balkans live in peace and security, that the sincere cooperation between the states goes ahead and be turned into an element of the progressive processes in Europe and in the world. This would be an important test for all those who speak about human rights of the individuals, about pluralism and democracy.[33]

Foto Çami said in an unusual statement that continued national oppression of Kosovars would adversely affect Tiranë-Belgrade relations. He added: "How can [Yugoslavia] seek to join the mainstream of Europe in the 21st century if it behaves in such a medieval way toward the Albanians, toward 2.5 million of its own citizens?"[34] Belgrade responded by accusing the Albanian government of fostering unrest in Kosovë.[35]

In contrast to the 1970s, Albania, and not Yugoslavia, appeared eager for cultural, economic, and even political cooperation and took the initiative to expand bilateral ties. Although prior to 1981 Yugoslavia had actively and persistently made great efforts to court Albania's friendship, by the end of the decade it did not seem to have a clear-cut policy toward Albania. While Foreign Ministry officials in Belgrade publicly declared that Yugoslavia attached great significance to Albania's pursuing an independent foreign policy and welcomed its expansion of relations with the outside world,[36] there were powerful forces at work in Belgrade that wished to see Albania remain isolated. Some Yugoslav officials, having quite incorrectly identified Albania as the main inciter of unrest in Kosovë, not only opposed the expansion of contacts with Albania but also advocated punitive actions against the country and mounted a concerted, highly focused attack on the PSRA's domestic and foreign policies. There were repeated threats from Belgrade to close down the Shkodër-Titograd railroad line—Albania's only rail link with the outside world—on grounds it was unprofitable. Suspension of the railway, which was of no particular economic importance to Yugoslavia, would have caused Albania considerable economic hardship.

The Albanians, recognizing the fluctuation and instability of their relations with Yugoslavia, tried to minimize the costs of potential punitive actions by intensifying interactions with other Balkan countries, particularly Greece, and Western Europe. Even though the future of relations between Albania and Yugoslavia appeared gloomy in the wake of the continuing deterioration of the situation in Kosovë, it was in their long-term economic, political, and security interests to find a modus vivendi. With Yugoslavia's deepening political and economic crisis and greater reliance on trade with the Soviet bloc, Albania was particularly concerned about its neighbor's vulnerability to Soviet pressures.

Greece and Turkey

By the late 1980s, Albania had achieved remarkable progress in strengthening ties with Greece. Although facing considerable domestic opposition, Andreas Papandreou's government engaged in wide-ranging discussions with Albania. For Greece, the main factor in improving ties was concern for the fate of some 58,000 ethnic Greeks in Albania. Athens had given up its territorial claims on southern Albania, apparently realizing that the lot of ethnic Greeks could improve only by cultivating a relationship of mutual trust between the two neighboring countries.

For Tiranë, the expansion of relations with Athens had become imperative both politically and economically. Yugoslavia had launched a coordinated media campaign against Albania, focusing attention on human rights abuses, particularly the alleged persecution of ethnic Greeks. In an attempt to drive a wedge between Tiranë and Athens, the Yugoslav media had given prominent coverage to anti-Albanian Greek nationalist activities.

Increased Yugoslav economic, military, and political pressures and support for what Albania considered Greek "reactionary forces" aroused suspicions in Tiranë of a possible Belgrade-Athens alliance—a recurring nightmare for the Albanians—and brought back memories of past Yugoslav-Greek discussions on partitioning Albania. In a posthumous book on Albanian-Greek relations published in July 1985, Hoxha set the tone for Tiranë's diplomatic shift toward Athens. He asserted that, faced with Yugoslav hostile actions, "we were obliged to and took the necessary defensive measures. . . . We were not going to allow the Titoites to act as they liked with our rights, to try to isolate us, to sabotage us as they did even by holding up our trucks which were transporting goods to the markets of Western Europe, and so on. This would have been impermissible."[37]

After a series of negotiations and exchanges of senior Foreign Ministry delegations, in the mid-1980s Albania and Greece signed a long-term economic agreement. In July 1985 the two countries signed a military protocol on the maintenance and repair of border markers and the prevention of border incidents. And in August 1987 Papandreou's government formally ended the state of war with Albania—an anomaly of World War II, when Italy had launched its invasion of Greece from occupied Albania. In announcing the lifting of the state of war, the Greek government emphasized its expectation that the decision would contribute to an improvement of the position of the Greek minority, which could serve as "a firm bridge of friendship between Hellenism and the Albanian people."[38] During a visit to Tiranë in November 1987, Greek Foreign Minister Karolos Papoulias signed a series of agreements, including a long-term agreement on economic, industrial, technical, and scientific cooperation; an agreement on expanding cultural exchanges; a four-year agreement for cooperation in the health sector; and a protocol on banking cooperation.[39] In April 1988 the two countries signed agreements on border trade and on the establishment of a ferry line between Corfu and Sarandë.

Albania's relations with Turkey did not expand as rapidly as those with Greece. Whereas bilateral relations were described by both sides as "excellent," Albania saw greater opportunities in cultivating ties with other countries. Although there were extensive cultural exchanges between the two nations, facilitated by the presence of as many as one million Albanians in Turkey, bilateral trade was not significant. Nevertheless, high-level contacts between Tiranë and Ankara continued to increase. Albania avoided taking a stand on Greek-Turkish disagreements in the Aegean Sea and was careful to play a balancing act.

Italy

In the post-1945 period Albania had developed closer relations with Italy than with any other Western country. Since the late 1960s,

Italy had been in the forefront of Western efforts to improve relations with Albania. The importance that Tiranë attached to the strengthening of ties with Rome became evident following Hoxha's death. In May 1985 Prime Minister Adil Çarçani sent a message to his Italian counterpart, Bettino Craxi, expressing Albania's desire for better cooperation between the two countries. Italy's Undersecretary of State for Foreign Affairs Bruno Corti was the first senior Western official to visit Tiranë after Hoxha's death.[40]

Italian hopes of serving as a Western link to Albania were dashed, at least temporarily, in late 1985 when six Albanian citizens sought refuge in the Italian embassy in Tiranë. The Albanian government demanded their unconditional surrender, but Italy insisted on assurances that the six would not be persecuted. Both sides were evidently interested in minimizing the impact of this incident on their overall relations, but bilateral cooperation was nevertheless adversely affected. The six remained in the Italian embassy, domestic concerns in both countries making it difficult to find a mutually acceptable solution.

RELATIONS WITH THE WEST

Although the expansion of external ties had been initiated before Hoxha's death, it was under Alia that the process of opening up toward the West was accelerated significantly. Alia evidently recognized that tackling economic problems required increased cooperation with other countries and technology imports, for which the West provided the best source. The regime apparently believed that its greatest possibilities lay in cooperation with Western Europe, particularly West Germany.

The leadership seemed concerned about Albania's bad image in the West because of its record on human rights. It embarked on a well-coordinated public relations campaign, increasing contacts with Western countries and permitting more Western officials, journalists, and private citizens to visit Albania. Although still highly suspicious of Western political and cultural influences, all indications suggested that under the Alia leadership the basic tenor of Albania's relationship with the West had significantly changed. Albania concluded long-term cultural and trade agreements with a number of Western European countries; it also increased political contacts with the West.

In September 1985 Tiranë welcomed French Deputy Foreign Minister Jean-Michel Baylet, the highest-ranking French official to visit Albania after 1945. The importance the Albanians attached to Baylet's visit was demonstrated in that he was received by Çarçani. Accompanied by a large group of Western executives interested in trade relations with the PSRA, Baylet held discussions with a number of senior officials. He was quoted as saying, "We talked in a very direct way, with no taboos whatsoever. . . . Subjects brought up included human rights."[41] At Albania's suggestion, a joint commission, composed of French industrialists and officials of the Albanian Chamber of Commerce, was established to study ways of expanding trade. In 1988 the two countries signed an agreement for economic, industrial, and technological cooperation and an agreement on cultural, scientific, and technological exchanges. In March 1989 Malile became the first Albanian foreign minister to pay an official visit to Paris in the post-1945 period. Both the French premier and the foreign minister accepted invitations to visit Tiranë. And Air France began flights to Tiranë, becoming the second Western airline (after Swissair) to fly to Albania.

In 1987 Albania established diplomatic relations with Canada and, of particular importance, with West Germany. For years, Tiranë had claimed reparations from Bonn for destruction in Albania during the German occupation in World War II, and in 1980 it threatened to take the case to the World Court. Albania's decision to drop these claims paved the way for the normalization of ties. Albania hoped that the establishment of relations with Bonn would open doors to much-needed advanced technology. West German Foreign Minister Hans-Dietrich Genscher was told, during a visit to Tiranë in October 1987, that Albania regarded West Germany as "its main economic partner of the future."[42] Albania reportedly expected West German assistance in modernizing its agriculture, exploiting its mineral resources, and modernizing its transportation system.[43] The major problem, however, was Albania's constitutional prohibition of foreign aid. Bavarian prime minister Franz-Josef Strauss, who had visited Tiranë several times before the establishment of ties between the countries, suggested that instead of granting formal credits, West Germany give Albania economic benefits by selling it goods at low prices. In November 1987 Strauss signed an aid accord in Tiranë by which Albania could purchase West German goods, with the exception of weapons and police vehicles, in the amount of DM 6 million.[44] An agreement signed in June 1988 provided for increased bilateral cooperation in the fields of industry, agriculture, energy, transportation, and construction. The Development Assistance Commmittee (DAC), an arm of the Organization for Economic Cooperation and Development (OECD), decided in December 1988 to list Albania as a less developed country, making it eligible to recieve economic assistance from OECD members. In March 1989 West Germany granted Albania DM 20 million in nonrepayable funds for development projects.[45] In accordance with the DAC decision, Japan also announced it would grant Albania development assistance.[46]

Albania's normalization of ties with Great Britain may turn out to be more difficult than that with West Germany. Albania demanded the return of its prewar gold reserves, looted by Nazi Germany and held in London since the end of the war. The British insisted that the Albanians first pay damages for the sinking of two British warships off Albania's coast in 1946—an incident for which Tiranë had denied responsibility, claiming it did not have mine-laying equipment at its disposal at the time. Tiranë resumed official discussions with London in March 1985. The talks reportedly continued off and on, with the Albanians insisting that ties would not be established until the gold was returned to Albania.

Albania held discussions with many Western firms about the purchase of modern industrial plants and the acquisition of advanced technology. It also sought technical assistance in locating and exploiting oil deposits on its coast and brought in Western experts to help supervise and operate imported technical equipment. Hundreds of students were sent for advanced training in the Western European countries, apparently in the hope of bridging an ever-widening gap between Albania's relatively nontechnical and rigid system and the increasingly complex and technologically advanced methods and development in the Western economies.

The barriers to substantial increases in Albanian foreign trade with the West remained daunting. One involved a critical shortage of foreign exchange, which had compelled Albania to resort to barter as payment in exchange for goods it imported. Export earnings had been adversely affected by the drastic decline of world prices for the raw materials Albania exported. Alia disclosed in 1986 that as a result of the drop in world prices of energy products Albania had lost between $40 and $45 million.[47] The limited number of export commodities that could effectively compete on the international market continued to present problems for officials charged with finding new ways of overcoming the foreign exchange crunch. The country's economic planning mechanism inhibited production of export commodities. Enterprises had little initiative to work better to augment the country's foreign currency earnings. An article in *Rruga e Partisë* suggested that the production of export commodities would be stimulated if enterprises were allowed to keep a proportion of the foreign currency earned through their exports.[48]

But the biggest hurdle to increased trade was the constitutional provision that prohibited the government from accepting foreign aid. Alia gave no indication that he was contemplating revising the self-reliance policy, although its disastrous impact on the nation's economic development had become perilously evident. But even with a significant jump in foreign trade and the possibility of renouncing Article 28 of the constitution, Albania still needed to restructure its economy, hamstrung by central planning, the diversion of investments to unprofitable projects, and the ban on private enterprise.

RELATIONS WITH THE SOVIET BLOC

After expanding ties with Western Europe and immediate neighbors, Alia turned his attention to relations with Albania's former Warsaw Pact allies, excluding the Soviet Union. In an important departure from Hoxha's policy of maintaining only commercial ties with Eastern Europe, Alia's government upgraded relations to the ambassadorial level with Bulgaria, Hungary, East Germany, and Czechoslovakia. Under Mikhail Gorbachev's leadership, the Soviet threat to Albania had receded, and the nation adopted a more flexible attitude toward its former allies. Albanian-Bulgarian relations improved remarkably, with frequent delegation exchanges at the ministerial level.

There was also a notable improvement in Tiranë–East Berlin relations. In June 1989 East German Foreign Minister Oskar Fischer became the first senior Soviet bloc official to visit Tiranë since the early 1960s. In an unusual gesture reflecting the importance the Albanians attached to cooperation with East Germany, Alia personally received Fischer. The East German news agency quoted Alia as having said that both countries were building "socialism" and that they held "identical" views on "important fundamental questions of our time."[49] After the break with China, Albanian leaders had maintained that Albania was the world's only "socialist" state. Alia acknowledged that East Germany, formerly treated as a "revisionist" state by the Albanian media, was also a "socialist" state, representing an important departure from Tiranë's previous ideological pronouncement. Both sides indicated there were no political obstacles to the expansion of bilateral ties. A number of important agreements were signed, providing for wide-ranging cooperation in industry, the exchange of know-how, and the training of Albanian specialists in East Germany.[50]

Long-term trade agreements for the period from 1986 to 1990 were signed with most Eastern European states. Before 1990, these countries had provided an important market for traditional Albanian exports and goods of inferior quality unsalable in Western markets. CMEA's decision to absorb huge amounts of Albania's shoddy manufactured goods and poor-quality food products was politically motivated in line with Moscow's policy of accommodation toward Albania. But Albania's trade with CMEA members was likely to suffer as East European countries move toward market economies. Tiranë will probably find it very difficult to convince these countries to continue barter trade with Albania at a time when they desperately need hard currency. Nevertheless, the East European revolution did not adversely affect Albania's relations with its former allies. The Albanian media provided unusually detailed and objective reporting on the upheaval in Eastern Europe. The Tiranë government was among the first to denounce former Romanian dictator Nicolaie Ceausescu and recognize the new government. While criticizing changes in East Europe on ideological grounds, the Albanian government was quick to distance itself from former East European communist regimes. Officials maintained that a similar upheaval could not occur in Albania because of the APL's "Marxist-Leninist policy." In a meeting of the Trade Unions Council in mid-December 1989, Alia said:

> There are people abroad who ask: Will processes like those taking place in East Europe also occur in Albania? We answer firmly and categorically: No, they will not occur in Albania. Why? Primarily, and above all else, because Albania is not the East. Albania and the European East have developed along completely different ideological, political, economic, and social roads. Therefore, the problems are not and cannot be the same. The crisis that is sweeping the countries in the East is the crisis of a definite community, the crisis of what used to be called the socialist community, but not the crisis of socialism as a theory and practice. Consequently, the events taking place over there have nothing to do with us.[51]

There was no change in Albania's attitude toward the USSR. In fact, Albania had become a harsh critic of Gorbachev's *perestroika* and *glasnost* policies. Moreover, Albania appeared to be concerned with what it interpreted as Soviet support for Serbia regarding the Kosovë issue. Whereas in the early 1980s the Soviet media had maintained a neutral position on Kosovë, providing only minimal coverage on developments in the troubled province, by 1989 coverage of the Albanian-Serbian conflict had increased, with a distinctly pro-Serbian bias.[52] On the other hand, the Soviets continued to call for the restoration of ties with Albania.

CONCLUSION

The most likely scenario for Albania's foreign policy in the 1990s appears to be a gradual but steady expansion of relations with both East and West. Although fanatically preserving its foreign policy independence, Albania will most likely reassess its policy of self-reliance. West Germany and Italy will probably become Albania's primary foreign trade partners and could provide Tiranë with badly needed technical and economic assistance. With the passage of time, the issues that in the past prevented Albania from restoring ties with the United States and the Soviet Union are likely to become less salient because the post-Hoxha leadership gave less importance to ideological intransigence, thus opening the way for the possible normalization of these relations. Ties with Yugoslavia are likely to remain strained, as there appear to be few prospects for a solution of the Kosovë problem.

Western policy should take advantage of Albania's opening to the outside world and domestic changes. Positive political, economic, and human rights developments ought to be rewarded with economic ties and support. In addition to helping Albania safeguard its independence and assist its economic development, one of the main Western objectives should be the promotion of greater pluralism and better human rights performances through expansion and broadening of dialogue and contacts with both the Albanian government and society.

Ja qifsha rrobt Serbit 2016

7

The Albanians in Yugoslavia

For seven days in March 1989, tens of thousands of ethnic Albanian demonstrators battled security forces throughout the province of Kosovë, once again drawing attention to the perennial problem of the more than two million–strong Albanian minority in Yugoslavia.[1] According to official reports, twenty-four people died and hundreds were injured.[2] Other sources claimed that more than one hundred people had died. The disturbances began March 23, when Kosovë's Assembly approved constitutional changes reducing the region's autonomy within the republic of Serbia. The 1974 constitution had given Kosovë and Vojvodina, Serbia's other province, considerable autonomy.

The Albanians had expressed opposition to the changes through massive peaceful protests and an unprecedented general strike. In November 1988 some 100,000 Albanians demonstrated in the provincial capital, Prishtinë. The demonstrators ostensibly took to the streets to express support for provincial leaders Azem Vllasi and Kaçusha Jashari, who had been ousted under Serbian pressure. But they brought to the surface Albanians' simmering hostility toward Slobodan Milošević, the Serb populist leader, who for more than two years had been waging an all-out crusade to bring Kosovë under Serbia's full control. The protestors displayed a remarkable political subtlety. They were well organized, did not resort to violence, and carried Tito's picture and the Yugoslav flag. They contrasted sharply with Serbian demonstrators, who at protest meetings throughout the summer of 1988 had used with impunity repulsive slogans such as "Death to Vllasi!" and "Death to the Albanians!" In February 1989 a protest by miners in Mitrovicë led to an unprecedented general strike, paralyzing Kosovë's economy. A petition signed by 215 Kosovar intellectuals appealed to the Serbian Assembly not to approve constitutional changes that would endanger Kosovë's autonomy, insisting that "Albanian protests against constitutional changes are legitimate." It warned that the curtailment of Kosovë's autonomy "would provoke the sincere feeling among Albanians that something has been taken away from them that was not given as a present but which has belonged to them from the very beginning."[3]

But disregarding the wishes of ethnic Albanians, Milošević persisted in his drive to bring Kosovë under Serbia's control. In late February 1989 a state of emergency was imposed and thousands of troops and special federal police units were dispatched to Kosovë. Milošević ordered the arrest of Vllasi and dozens of other prominent Albanians, blaming them for the demonstrations and strikes in Kosovë, and engineered the selection of former provincial police chief Rrahman Morina as new Kosovë party leader. The Kosovë Assembly approved the constitutional changes literally under the barrel of the gun: Before casting their votes, Albanian deputies, according to Yugoslav and foreign media reports, were interrogated by the secret police. Although only days before the Kosovë Assembly session a Serbian provincial official had said changes were not likely to be approved, in the end, with the assembly building surrounded by tanks and MIG-21 fighters flying low over Prishtinë, out of 180 delegates only ten voted against and two abstained. No ethnic group in Europe had been subjected to such outright intimidation since Stalin's subjugation of Eastern Europe in the 1940s.

The March 1989 clashes were the first violent Albanian demonstrations in eight years. In April 1981 the Yugoslav government had dispatched the army to Kosovë to put an end to ethnic Albanian unrest caused by a rising spirit of nationalism that stemmed from political and economic grievances, anti-Serb sentiments, and dissatisfaction with perceived indifference to Kosovar needs on the part of the rest of Yugoslavia. The government clamped down on Albanian activists demanding that Kosovë be proclaimed a republic within the Yugoslav federation. More than 1,300 Albanians, the majority of them youths, were sentenced to prison terms of up to fifteen years for "counterrevolutionary" activity; some 6,000 were convicted of misdemeanor charges; and an undisclosed number of officials, teachers, and workers lost their jobs. In October 1988 the Prishtinë daily, Rilindja, quoted Morina, then Kosovë police chief, as saying that since 1981 some 485,000 Albanians "had passed through the hands of the police." Whereas Albanians represented only 8 percent of Yugoslavia's population, they accounted for 70 percent of the country's political prisoners.

By the late 1980s, the rights of ethnic Albanians were eroding at a discouraging rate. Paradoxically, the increased repression of Albanians occurred at a time of significant liberalization and democratization in other parts of Yugoslavia, particularly in Slovenia and Croatia. Yugoslav non-Serbs and foreigners generally failed to understand some of the harsh realities of what came to be known as the Kosovë drama. Western governments, sensitive to Yugoslavia's geopolitical position and delicate internal situation, largely ignored human rights transgressions against Albanians. Whereas similar acts of repression against minorities in other socialist countries, such as China, the Soviet Union, and Romania, had been denounced in no uncertain terms, the repression of Kosovars drew only minimal rebuke, mainly by the Western press.

The approval of constitutional changes represented the culmination of Serbia's virulent campaign to restrict Kosovë's autonomy by accusing the Albanians of persecuting local Slavs. Through the manipulation of mass street gatherings of Serbs and Montenegrins, inflammatory media coverage, and political smear campaigns, Milošević had monopolized Yugoslavia's decisionmaking process regarding the Albanian question. He subverted, distorted, and defeated Albanian efforts to secure full equality with the country's other major ethnic groups. A well-coordinated, Serbian-inspired media campaign had led to a dramatic increase in anti-Albanian sentiment in Serbia, Macedonia, and Montenegro. Claiming Albanian discrimination, the Serbian and Montenegrin minority, beginning in spring 1986, had staged massive protest meetings in the province, which eventually spread to Serbia, the province of Vojvodina, and Montenegro. Responsible officials, including Milošević, accused the Albanians of carrying out "genocide" against Serbs and Montenegrins. Officials spoke ominously of the dangers Albanians represented and the necessity to settle accounts once and for all with what they invariably described as Albanian "nationalists and irredentists." A lingering perception was created both at home and abroad of Albanian irredentism bent on the destruction of Yugoslavia and horrendous mistreatment of local Serbs—a view that reflected the image so fiercely promoted by the Milošević-controlled media.

The Albanian problem was further complicated by extreme social and economic inequalities. Kosovë had become the most densely populated region in Yugoslavia and the authorities were concerned by sharply differential ethnic growth. Albanian birthrates remained very high, whereas those of the Serbs, Macedonians, and Montenegrins were low. According to the April 1981 census, there were about 1,730,000 Albanians in Yugoslavia, of whom 1,227,424 lived in Kosovë, 377,000 in Macedonia, 72,432 in Serbia proper, and 37,735 in Montenegro. In Kosovë, the Albanians represented 77.5 percent of the total population, in Macedonia 19.8 percent, and in Montenegro 6.4 percent. There were 206,000 Serbs and Montenegrins, representing about 15 percent of the total population of Kosovë.[5] On the national level, the Albanians in 1981 had already outnumbered the Macedonians (1,340,000) and the Montenegrins (577,298), and were rapidly catching up to the Slovenes (1,750,000) and ethnic Moslems (2,000,000). Proportionally, there were more Albanians in Kosovë (77.5 percent) than Croatians (75 percent),

Macedonians (67 percent), and Montenegrins (68.5 percent) in their respective republics. In 1987 the birthrate in Kosovë was 29.9 per thousand, compared with 11.5 in Vojvodina, 12.6 in Serbia, 12.8 in Croatia, and 14.2 in Slovenia.[6] More than 50 percent of the population were under the age of twenty-seven. Yugoslavia's next census, scheduled for 1991, is likely to confirm that the Albanians have become the country's third largest ethnic group. According to Yugoslav demographers, high birthrates are likely to continue. The population of Kosovë appeared to be exceptionally marriage-minded. According to one source, almost the entire adult population was married, the divorce rate was lower than in other parts of the country, and the childbearing period was relatively long.[7] Demographers have predicted that by the year 2000 Kosovë will have 2.5 million residents and by 2021, 3.5 million.[8]

Albanians remained the poorest and least integrated ethnic group in Yugoslavia. Kosovë was characterized by conditions of extreme economic underdevelopment, diminishing opportunities for upward mobility, general social malaise, and deteriorating living standards. There appeared to be a widespread perception among the Kosovars that Serbia and the central government were to blame for the socioeconomic deprivations and the lamentable state of affairs. Despite considerable federal assistance during the 1970s and the 1980s, the gap between economic conditions in Kosovë and other regions had widened. The unbalanced regional investment policy, which had neglected processing and manufacturing industries, had done little to alleviate the acute poverty of the average Albanian. A large number of people, little affected by the significant socioeconomic transformations that Kosovë had undergone in the post-1945 era, continued to live in conditions of poverty, exploitation, and hopelessness. In 1988 the per capita annual income in Kosovë amounted to only 29 percent of the Yugoslav average. The province had the highest inflation and the lowest employment rates in the country. Unemployment seemed to be the most serious and intractable problem. The expansion of mass education had produced an army of educated people who had no career opportunities. In 1989 there were some 150,000 people registered as unemployed. But the actual number ran closer to several hundred thousands because many people, aware that they could not get work, apparently did not register at the appropriate office. A major segment of the population was reportedly on the verge of starvation as 65,000 families had no source of income.[9] That 75 percent of the unemployed were young people under twenty-seven years of age, most of them well educated, was of serious concern to the authorities.[10] With an annual influx of 25,000 people into the working population, unemployment was likely to threaten the social fabric of the Kosovar society. Some 366,000 new jobs would have to be created by the year 2000 to keep unemployment at approximately the level of 1988.[11] Out of desperation, many Albanians chose to migrate either to other parts of Yugoslavia or to Western Europe and the United States. Between 1974 and 1988, some 250,000 Albanians had migrated from Kosovë, Macedonia, and Montenegro.[12]

Kosovë was characterized by ethnic imbalances. The Serbian and Montenegrin minority (who made up 15 percent of the population as a whole) continued to wield disproportionate political and economic power. In 1978 some 20 percent of Kosovë Assembly delegates were Serbs and Montenegrins, whereas 72.6 percent were Albanians.[13] In 1982 Albanians accounted for 53.5 percent of the total number of workers with special authority and responsibilities, the Serbs and Montenegrins accounting for 38.8 percent. Of Kosovë's 251 presidents of administrative agencies of sociopolitical organizations, 54.3 percent were Albanians, and 37.8 percent Serbs and Montenegrins.[14] In 1983 the national structure of workers in Kosovë's administrative organs was as follows: Albanians 448 (61 percent), Serbs and Montenegrins 260 (32.5 percent), and others 52 (6.5 percent).[15] Of the total 2,484 deputies in district assemblies, 20.5 percent (511) were Serbs and Montenegrins, and 74 percent (1,839) Albanians.[16] The national structure of secretaries of basic party organizations elected in 1982 also reflected the underrepresentation of Albanians, who accounted for 72.3 percent, Serbs and Montenegrins 26 percent. The Kosovë League of Communists had about 102,000 members in the mid-1980s, 67 percent Albanians, 27.7 percent Serbs and Montenegrins. In the provincial party committee, 70.5 percent were Albanians and 24.2 percent Serbs and Montenegrins.[17] Of the 140,000 people employed in the social sector in 1985, Albanians accounted for 68.4 percent, and Serbs and Montenegrins 25.8 percent.[18]

The national structure of the unemployed people also indicated that Albanians were worst off: They accounted for 79.8 percent of the registered unemployed, with Serbs and Montenegrins making up 14.5 percent.[19] Although only 26.9 percent of Albanians occupied state-owned apartments in 1987, the figure for the Serbs was 70 percent, and for the Montenegrins close to 85 percent.[20] The situation of Albanians in Macedonia was even more unfavorable. Whereas in 1981 Albanians represented close to 20 percent of Macedonia's population, they accounted for only 6.7 percent of the people employed in the social sector; the Macedonians accounted for 82.8 percent.[21]

The issue of Kosovë, a constant irritant in Tiranë-Belgrade relations, was also of serious concern to Albania. Ramiz Alia's government was faced with a daunting dilemma: It was painfully caught between its desire and the necessity to maintain good relations with Yugoslavia— its most important neighbor—and its sympathy and allegiance to ethnic Albanians. Although the substance of its policy toward Yugoslavia had not essentially changed after 1981, Albania did officially endorse Kosovar demands for a republic. This drew Yugoslav charges that Albania was inciting the Kosovars. The Yugoslavs did not provide any credible evidence to support their allegations, and by most accounts the Albanian government, preoccupied with its own formidable domestic problems, was not playing on Kosovars' nationalist feelings. But from the Yugoslav standpoint the threat was not so much what Albania did but what it represented for the Kosovars—their mother country.

THE ROOTS OF THE PROBLEM

Albanian nationalism in Yugoslavia did not appear suddenly in the early 1980s. It had deep historical, social, and economic roots that helped mold contemporary Kosovar identity. The poignancy of the Kosovë problem could in no way be denied; Kosovë evoked strong passions that had kept tensions between the two groups at high but, at least until the late 1980s, manageable levels. For the Serbs, Kosovë represented the mystical symbol of Serbdom. The region was part of the medieval Serbian state, and Pejë (Peć) the seat of the Serbian Patriarchate.

Serbian scholars' idiosyncratic excursions through history maintained that Albanians were "newcomers" to Kosovë, having moved into the region with the encouragement of Ottoman authorities after the Serbian exodus in the wake of the Austrian-Ottoman wars of 1689–1690 and 1737–1739. The Serbs insisted that during the Balkan Wars in 1912, Kosovë was "liberated" by the Serbian army and that thereafter the Albanians enjoyed all the freedoms and liberties accorded national minorities. In the late 1980s, the Serbs also claimed that hundreds of thousands of people from Albania had moved across the border into Kosovë during and after World War II.[22] The implication was that Enver Hoxha, in accordance with his designs on Kosovë, had sent thousands of people there after the 1948 break between Yugoslavia and the Soviet Union. This argument had become widespread, although figures released in 1987 by the Yugoslav Ministry of Internal Affairs indicated that after 1948 only about 6,000 Albanians had escaped from Albania into Yugoslavia. About 5,500 of them eventually left Yugoslavia, settling in Western Europe and the United States.[23]

The Albanians, for their part, argued that it was precisely the Serbs' unwillingness to accept them as equals in their midst and having imposed on them a subordinate position that had been at the root of the Serbian-Albanian conflict for seven decades. Albanian historians rejected the Serbian agument that the Albanians first settled in Kosovë during the seventeenth and eighteenth centuries, insisting that the Albanians represented an autochthonous ethnic group that constituted the majority of Kosovë's population even before the seventeenth century. But on contemporary historical grounds, Albanians made an even better case. Whereas the Serbs, who by the end of the 1980s composed less than 10 percent of the province's population, based their claims primarily on a legendary myth of a bygone era, Albanians pointed to Kosovë's central place in their own modern history. Kosovë was the cradle of Albanian nationalism, and the Kosovars had played a prominent role in the nationalist movements of the late nineteenth and early twentieth centuries and in the struggle that led to the proclamation of Albania's independence in 1912. The Serbs were able to impose their control over Kosovë and annex it from Albania only through force and with the sanction of the Great Powers.

Under Yugoslav rule Kosovë has had a torturous history. Yugoslavs always considered Albanians, who had a distinct and well-developed national consciousness and never willingly participated in their annexation to Yugoslavia, to be outsiders. They made great efforts to dismantle the fabric of Albanian culture and society. In the process of pacifying Kosovë following its partition from Albania in 1912, the Serbian and Montenegrin armies committed large-scale atrocities against the indigenous population.[24] Even after their violent conquest, the Kosovars retained a strong sense of nationalism, and armed resistance against Serbian authorities continued until the late 1920s.[25] Belgrade pursued a policy of colonialism, and ethnic Albanians were subjected to forced assimilation and denationalization. Kosovë and other compact Albanian-inhabited areas were divided into different administrative units. Albanians were not recognized as a distinct ethnic group, the use of the Albanian language was prohibited, and Albanians in large numbers were forced to change their names by adding the Serbian suffixes -vić and -ić. The authorities used agrarian reform as a means of transforming Kosovë into a predominantly Serbian province and forcing the Albanians to emigrate to Turkey and Albania.[26] By 1941 more than 500,000 Kosovars had been forced to leave their native land, and some 40,000 Slav colonists had been settled in the Albanian-inhabited areas.[27] In the words of the Serbian constitutional scholar Radošin Rajević, the Albanians were "subjected to cruel national oppression" and "did not even enjoy the most elementary national and civic rights."[28]

Despite the harsh persecution and efforts forcibly to assimilate and denationalize the Albanians, Kosovars' ethnic consciousness and assertiveness grew. This prompted the Yugoslav diplomat Vaso Čubrilović to recommend a "final solution" to the Albanian problem. In a memorandum of March 1937 to the royal government, Čubrilović argued that "the only means to cope with [the Albanians] is the brute force of an organized state." He recommended the deportation of the entire Albanian population from southern Yugoslavia to Albania and Turkey.[29]

In the wake of Yugoslavia's dismemberment in 1941, Kosovë was reunited with Albania. Many Serbs left Kosovë. Significantly, despite the repression in the 1920s and the 1930s, during the war there were no mass atrocities by Albanians against the Serbs in Kosovë. In fact, Albanians provided protection to local Serbs against the Italians and the Germans.

THE YCP AND THE ALBANIAN QUESTION

Between the wars, the Yugoslav Communist Party (YCP) had condemned the persecution of Albanians and had twice endorsed the return of Kosovë and other Albanian-inhabited regions to Albania: at its Fourth Congress, held in Dresden in 1928, and at its Fifth Conference, held in Zagreb in 1940.[30] During the war, a Communist-dominated partisan movement was organized. The YCP recognized the right of ethnic Albanians to self-determination, including secession. The Kosovë branch of the YCP and the partisan movement were independent of the party and partisan movement in Serbia and until the end of the war maintained direct links with the YCP Central Committee.[31]

The Communists encountered considerable problems enlisting the support of Albanian masses. With fresh memories of harsh persecution in the interwar period and fearing that a Communist victory would lead to Kosovë's reincorporation into Yugoslavia, many Kosovars opposed the Yugoslav partisan movement. Nevertheless, Kosovar Communists were able to organize a partisan movement, which by the end of the war numbered about 53,000 armed men. Partisan leaders pledged that at the end of the war the Kosovars would be given the opportunity to freely exercise their right to self-determination. Fadil Hoxha, commander of the General Staff of Kosovë, maintained at the time that if the Communists came to power in both Albania and Yugoslavia, then the question of Kosovë "would be resolved in a Marxist way." Because "in Kosovë and Metohija the majority are Albanians," though, he believed that it would "certainly . . . go to Albania."[32] Moreover, Kosovë's union with Albania was endorsed by the first conference of the Provincial People's Council of Kosovë, which was held from December 31, 1943, to January 2, 1944, at Bujan, northern Albania. The Bujan Resolution, which in the 1980s would become the subject of tremendous controversy, left no doubt regarding the preferences of Kosovar partisan leaders:

> Kosovë and the Dukagjin Plateau is a region that is predominantly inhabited by Albanians, who as always, today too, desire to unite with Albania.

Therefore, we consider it out duty to show the correct road which the Albanian people must take in order to realize its aspirations. The only way for the union of Albanians of Kosovë and the Dukagjin Plateau with Albania is through a joint struggle with the other peoples of Yugoslavia, against the occupier and its henchmen, because that is the only way to regain freedom, when all the peoples, including the Albanians, will have the opportunity to decide their fate, through the right of self-determination including secession. A guarantee of this is the National Liberation Army of Yugoslavia, and the National Liberation Army of Albania with which it is closely linked. Furthermore, a guarantee of this are our great allies: The Soviet Union, Great Britain and America (the Atlantic Charter, the Moscow and Teheran Conferences).[33]

The Yugoslav Communists were on the eve of coming to power after having defeated the Serb-dominated Chetnic nationalist movement. They were eager not to further alienate the Serbs. Allowing Kosovë to reunite with Albania would have represented a serious blow to Serbian nationalism and would have resulted in the loss of the support of the largest ethnic group in Yugoslavia, without whose acquiescence the Communists probably could not maintain power. In March 1944 the Yugoslav party Central Committee rejected the Bujan Resolution, thereby sealing the future of Kosovë.[34] And in a meeting with Enver Hoxha in July 1946, Tito ruled out the possibility of allowing Kosovë to reunite with Albania. He reportedly told Hoxha that "Kosovë and the other regions inhabited by Albanians belong to Albania and that we shall return them to you, but not now because the great-Serb reaction would not actually accept such a thing."[35]

During the last stage of the war, Albanian and Yugoslav partisans cooperated closely. Party cadres from Albania were sent to Kosovë and Macedonia. At the request of the High Command of the Yugoslav National Liberation Army in September 1944, the ACP agreed to dispatch to Kosovë two army divisions, consisting of over 20,000 men. Albanian partisan units played an important military as well as political role in pacifying Kosovë.

In late 1944, under the pretext of destroying "enemy" remnants, the Yugoslav army undertook a massive campaign in the Albanian regions. As a result, an open revolt broke out in Kosovë. Before the very eyes of their "comrades in arms" from Albania, Yugoslav partisans committed unprecedented atrocities against the Albanian population. According to Albanian sources, during late 1944 and early 1945 about 10,000 Albanians were arrested in Tetovë, Macedonia, of whom 1,200 were executed. Some 2,000 Albanian recruits were allegedly executed upon reaching Bar, Montenegro. In addition, 2,000 Albanian recruits, most of them from Macedonia, were reportedly killed by poisonous gas at Gorica, near Trieste.[36] The Albanians were the only national minority group that put up an armed resistance, which lasted until 1948, against the Yugoslav Communist regime. Yugoslav sources provide few details on the Albanian revolt. Albania's Communist authorities have asserted that between 1945 and 1948, 36,000 Kosovars were murdered.[37] Albanian émigré sources, on the other hand, claim that as many as 60,000 ethnic Albanians perished during those years.[38]

KOSOVË, 1945–1966

The end of the war saw the reincorporation of Kosovë and other Albanian areas into Yugoslavia. Despite the many pledges made by the YCP during the war, ethnic Albanians were denied the right of self-determination and equality with other ethnic groups of Yugoslavia. The constitutional arrangements concerning Albanian territories were decided arbitrarily and without reference to the wishes of the local population. Contrary to the official Yugoslav interpretation that Kosovë joined Serbia "according to the freely expressed will of the population,"[39] the fate of the province was decided in a meeting that Kosovë representatives Fadil Hoxha and Miladin Popović held in Belgrade in February 1945 with senior Yugoslav officials Edvard Kardelj, Aleksandar Ranković, Milovan Djilas, and Svetozar Vukmanović Tempo. According to Fadil Hoxha, they discussed several possible options, including Kosovë's union with Albania. Kardelj reportedly said that internal and external factors made it impossible to annex Kosovë to Albania. The meeting concluded that Kosovë would be attached to Serbia. Nevertheless, later both Kosovë leaders and scholars accepted the official interpretation which had the implication that if the Kosovars had voluntarily joined Serbia, they could at some point again voluntarily and based on the principle of self-determination decide to leave Serbia. The principle of self-determination, which Albanians unsuccessfully employed to convince Belgrade to grant Kosovë the status of a republic, continued to haunt the Serbs.

Albanians were considered by the central authorities to be politically unreliable; in order to play down the forces of Albanian nationalism, Albanian-compact territories were again divided along different administrative units. Southwestern areas bordering on Albania were incorporated into the republic of Montenegro. Tetovë, Dibër, and other southeastern areas became part of the republic of Macedonia. Kosovë was renamed Kosovë-Metohija (Kosmet) and was proclaimed an *oblast* (autonomous region) within the republic of Serbia. This, however, did not mean that Kosovars were granted autonomy but, rather, special status within Serbia. Kosovë did not even have the same status and rights as Vojvodina, the other autonomous unit of Serbia. Vojvodina was proclaimed an autonomous *province*: Its governmental structure was similar to that of a republic, it had a Supreme Court, and its highest governmental body was the People's Assembly. In contrast, the governmental structure of the autonomous *region* of Kosovë resembled that of local administrative units: It had no Supreme Court, and its highest governmental body was the People's Council. There were also differences in Kosovë's and Vojvodina's representation in federal bodies. Belgrade was in charge of all decisions, including those of purely local concern. Kosovë's autonomy was thus restricted primarily to the field of policy-execution rather than policymaking.[40]

In subjecting Albanian areas to gerrymandering, the Yugoslav regime sacrificed the national aspirations of ethnic Albanians, accommodating the nationalist goals of other Slav ethnic groups and giving a territorial and demographic consistency to the republics of Montenegro and Macedonia. From Belgrade's point of view, the division of Albanian territories was also desirable as it made it easier to maintain control over this non-Slav ethnic group and to check the rise of Albanian nationalism and irredentism.[41] These new administrative arrangements, however, hindered the process of ethnic Albanians' integration. Albanian nationalism might have developed along different lines had the Albanians in 1945 been granted equality with other ethnic groups, included into one territorial unit, and had Kosovë been given the status of a constituent republic. Nevertheless, in comparison with the interwar period, the position and status of ethnic Albanians improved considerably during a brief period after 1945. For the first time under Yugoslav rule, the Albanians were recognized as a distinct ethnic group and Albanian-language schools were opened in Kosovë and, to a lesser extent, in Macedonia and Montenegro.

Between 1945 and 1948, the Yugoslavs dominated Tiranë's domestic and foreign affairs and hoped to solve the Kosovë problem through Albania's incorporation into the Yugoslav federation. This plan, however, was thwarted with the Tito-Stalin break and Albania's alliance with the Soviet Union. The APL purged itself of those Communists who had close links with Belgrade. Albania became Yugoslavia's harshest critic within the Communist bloc and launched a fierce propaganda campaign against Belgrade's domestic and foreign policies. Post-1948 tensions between Tiranë and Belgrade were usually accompanied by Yugoslav acts of repression against the Kosovars. The exercise of power in Albanian areas lay in the hands of Serbs, Montenegrins, and Macedonians, who employed political means at their disposal, especially the secret police, to preserve their dominant positions. Albanians were accorded the status of second-class citizens, and their access to political, economic, and social resources was extremely limited. The role of the autonomous

region of Kosovë was reduced to that of an administrative unit. Under
the direction of Vice-President Aleksander Ranković, Kosovë was treated
as a mere Serbian colony.

Albanians became subject to renewed pressures of assimilation and
denationalization. Most Albanian-language schools in Macedonia and
Montenegro were closed. Serbo-Croatian and Macedonian languages
were accorded the status of "national languages," with Albanian not
given equal status even in Kosovë, where ethnic Albanians constituted
the majority of the population. The cultural development of the Albanians
was severely impaired and the training of Albanian experts was seriously
undermined. Drastic measures were taken against the thin stratum of
Albanian intelligentsia, especially teachers of Albanian language and
history, who were suspected of attempting to arouse the national consciousness of the Albanians. The display of Albanian national symbols
or the commemoration of national holidays was prohibited, and the
teaching of Albanian history, traditions, literature, and even folklore was
considered "a nationalist deviation."[42]

In line with its assimilation policy, the Yugoslav government de-
liberately attempted to shape the ethnic Albanians into a separate and
distinct nation from their conationals in Albania, although Albanians
on both sides of the border considered themselves a single nation.
Albanians in Yugoslavia were referred to as *šiptari*, their conationals in
Albania as *albanci*. Attempts toward the development of a standardized
Albanian language were discouraged. Yugoslav authorities maintained
that Albanians in Yugoslavia, who were not permitted contacts with
their mother country, were being socialized in the "self-management"
system and in the spirit of *bratstvo i jedinstvo* (brotherhood and unity)
and would eventually develop a new national consciousness. But these
attempts to create a separate Albanian ethnonational entity only bred
resentment among ethnic Albanians and deterred their integration into
the Yugoslav mainstream.

Belgrade's misguided policies toward ethnic Albanians were carried
to an extreme by Ranković, who also was in charge of the secret police.
Under the pretext of fighting Albanian nationalism and irredentism, the
secret police pursued a campaign of intimidation against the Albanians.
Secret police officials interfered in all aspects of life and maintained files
on about 120,000 suspected Albanians.[43] On many occasions, most
notably during "the arms collection campaign" of 1956, they employed
violence and terror, including the murder of many Albanians ostensibly
suspected of nationalist activities.[44] More than in any other part of
Yugoslavia, members of the secret police in Kosovë were involved in
serious transgressions of the law. The secret police also pressured the

Albanians to emigrate. Between 1953 and 1957 alone some 195,000 Albanians emigrated, most of them from Kosovë and Macedonia. By 1966 about 230,000 Kosovars had left Yugoslavia.[45]

Albanians during this period were also discriminated against in the economic sphere. Development of Kosovë and other areas inhabited by Albanians, noted for their unmitigated economic backwardness, was given no priority by the Yugoslav authorities. The compelling motives seem to have been of a political nature. The contribution of the Albanian ethnic group to the Communist victory was considered minimal, and Belgrade saw no urgency in providing assistance to Kosovë. Furthermore, following the break with the Soviet bloc and the exacerbation of relations between Belgrade and Tiranë, areas bordering on Albania were thought to be too vulnerable as sites for the construction of industrial projects. Although Kosovë was clearly the most underdeveloped region in Yugoslavia, until the late 1950s it was not listed as such and was not eligible for special development funds. After 1958 the government granted assistance, but it was insufficient to accelerate the region's development. Investments per capita in Kosovë were considerably below the Yugoslav average. Thus, during the period between 1947 and 1956, gross investments per capita were 36 percent of the Yugoslav average, and between 1957 and 1965, 59.1 percent.[46] The region was also hindered in developing a diversified economy. Kosovë was relatively rich in mineral resources and investments were primarily concentrated into the extractive industry, making the region essentially a raw-material supplier for the manufacturing and processing industries concentrated in the northern, developed republics. Kosovë had over 20 percent of Yugoslavia's known coal deposits, over 60 percent of lead and zinc reserves, 58 percent of lignite deposits, and 50 percent of ferronickel ore.[47] Even during the 1970s, when Belgrade made genuine efforts to intensify Kosovë's economic development by pouring in large sums of aid, investments continued to be concentrated in the extractive industries.[48] A noted Kosovar sociologist, Hivzi Islami, asserted that this investment policy was motivated by the needs of Yugoslavia's overall industrial development and not those of Kosovë.[49] The primary beneficiaries of these investments were not the Kosovars but rather the country's richer republics, which prompted Kosovars to complain of exploitation. In an article published in April 1982, Kosovar veteran journalist Zenun Çelaj complained that although Kosovë was interested in the construction of industrial projects where it could process its raw materials and thus create greater employment opportunities, other republics and Vojvodina province were interested primarily in obtaining raw materials and energy resources from that region.[50]

DEMANDS FOR AN ALBANIAN REPUBLIC

Throughout the 1950s and the early 1960s, relations between Albanians and Serbs appeared to be harmonious on the surface. But there were latent Albanian hostility toward the Serbs and sporadic calls for the establishment of an Albanian republic within the Yugoslav federation. The government responded harshly to any sign of a resurgence of Albanian nationalism.

The euphoria that characterized Yugoslavia following Ranković's dismissal in 1966 encouraged Albanian intellectuals and political elite to express their aspirations for greater cultural and political autonomy. Mass education had the unintended effect of accentuating ethnic differences between Albanians and Serbs. As public education spread, increasing numbers of Albanians became keenly aware of their national identity and language, their stormy history, and, perhaps more important, their subordinate position in the Yugoslav federation. Kosovë and other Albanian-inhabited regions experienced a cultural revival, expressed through the glorification of the past, the promotion of national themes and symbols, and the rejection of the Serbian interpretation of Albanian history and its verdict on Kosovar movements and national heroes who had achieved prominence in the struggle against the Serbian "bourgeoisie." Firmly controlled before 1966, Kosovar scholars took advantage of the more liberal atmosphere to write Kosovë's history from a distinctive, Albanian point of view, emphasizing the existence and past unity of the Albanian nation.

The new freedom to glorify their past and express pride in national achievements was accompanied by a resurgence of nationalism and an exacerbation of ethnic antagonism throughout Albanian-inhabited regions. Kosovars demanded an improvement in their sociopolitical status and economic conditions; an end to the policy of discrimination against them in government, education, and economic activity; and proportional representation in local and federal government. They rejected Serbian implications that they were not fit to run their own affairs. They employed the principle of self-determination in an attempt to convince Belgrade to grant Kosovë republican status. At a session of the Socialist Alliance of Working People of Serbia in April 1968, Mehmet Hoxha, a distinguished partisan hero, raised what ethnic Albanians considered a legitimate question: "Why do 370,000 Montenegrins have their own republic, while 1.2 million Albanians do not even have total autonomy?"[51] At the September 1968 session of the provincial party committee, a group of Albanian intellectuals demanded that the right to self-determination of the Albanian ethnic group be recognized and that Kosovë be elevated to a republic. They insisted that only through the creation of a separate republic could Albanians achieve full equality. This view was supported by many Kosovar officials, including the provincial prosecutor, Rezhak Shala.[52]

As the Albanians pushed ahead with demands for reform, local Serbs and Montenegrins expressed deep suspicions about the effects of granting the Kosovars full equality. They viewed with skepticism and apprehension demands for the change of the status quo in Kosovë and insisted on the legitimacy and maintenance of existing arrangements, arguing that the national question had been "solved."

In late 1968 demonstrations broke out in Kosovë and western Macedonia. The demonstrators demanded the creation of a Kosovar republic, the establishment of an independent Albanian university, equal status for Albanian and Serbo-Croatian languages, and more jobs for Albanians. The authorities used force to quell the protests. Tito apparently had contemplated granting Kosovë republican status but gave up the idea because of strong Serbian opposition.[53] Following the demonstrations, however, Belgrade granted the Kosovars more national rights and took measures to improve their sociopolitical position. The 1969 and 1971 constitutional amendments and later the 1974 constitution gave Kosovë considerable autonomy. Although denied the political decision-making autonomy enjoyed by the republics, the province was recognized as "a constituent element" of the federation. An Albanian university was founded; a provincial Supreme Court was established; and the equality of Albanian, Serbo-Croatian, and Turkish languages was recognized. For the first time since 1945, the Albanians were allowed to display national emblems, including their flag. With the introduction of the "national key" form of representation, the Albanians obtained greater representation in local, republican, and federal government institutions. Measures were also taken to narrow the ethnic imbalances in all spheres of life in Kosovë, thus contributing to the elevation of the overall position of the Albanians. The position of Albanians outside Kosovë, however, improved only modestly. The authorities in Montenegro and Macedonia were slow to ensure Albanians equal economic, cultural, and political opportunities. Very few Albanians were appointed to high party, government, and administrative positions. In both republics, but especially in Macedonia, the Albanians continued to be severely oppressed.

With the improvement of relations between Albania and Yugoslavia, following the Soviet invasion of Czechoslovakia, direct contacts were established between Tiranë and Prishtinë. Belgrade assigned Kosovë the role of "bridge-building" with Albania, a part the Kosovars were eager to play. Cultural cooperation between universities in Tiranë and Kosovë flourished. Albanian textbooks and other educational materials were imported from Albania and professors from Tiranë University began lecturing at Kosovë University. Contacts with Albania and exposure to an ever-growing number of Albanian-language publications, radio, and television reinforced traditional bonds among Albanians on both sides of the border.

Meanwhile, a new, self-confident, political and cultural elite emerged and gradually, but persistently, began to challenge what the Albanians considered outdated political arrangements. In 1971 the provincial party chief, Veli Deva, was replaced by Mahmut Bakalli. Many of the older party and government officials were sent into semiretirement or named as provincial representatives in Belgrade. As participants in the power structure, members of the new elite aimed at maximizing Kosovë's autonomy within the existing system. Relying on the national base as a source of legitimacy, Bakalli used the ethnic issue to increase Kosovë's autonomy and employed the pronouncements of the Yugoslav League of Communists (YLC) on "brotherhood and unity" to advocate the full recognition of ethnic Albanians' national rights. Although the Albanians had made considerable progress in their national self-assertion and social, economic, and political development, argued Bakalli, further efforts would have to be made to promote their "equality of rights."[54] Pursuing a hard-line policy toward suspected "nationalists and irredentists," Bakalli nevertheless effectively used nationalist sentiments as a bureaucratic instrument of pressure to obtain greater autonomy from Serbia. He argued that the situation in Kosovë could get out of hand and thus cause unforeseen problems if the Albanians were not granted more autonomy.[55] Bakalli also embarked upon a policy of rapid expansion of education and permitted greater expression of nationalist sentiment, which led to an explosion in the publication of works exalting Albanian culture and history.

Albanians' self-assertion brought them into open conflict with the Serbs, who were alarmed at the gains the Kosovars were making. Seeing their political power decline, Serbs and Montenegrins felt threatened in the new environment, charged that they were being discriminated against, and complained that the federal government had granted Albanians "too many concessions." The Serbs were particularly concerned that their numbers in Kosovë were dwindling while at the same time the ethnic Albanian population was rapidly growing. According to the 1971 census, Kosovë had a population of 1,243,693, of whom 916,168 (or 73.6) percent were Albanians, 228,264 (or 18.3 percent) Serbs, and 33,000 (or 2.5 percent) Montenegrins.[56] Stiff competition for scarce jobs and apartments in the ever-growing urban areas further aggravated the ethnic conflict. Although Kosovë underwent social and economic transformations and received substantial assistance from the federal government throughout the 1970s, it remained the least developed area. Despite promises of narrowing the gap between Kosovë and other areas, the system generated greater inequalities. Moreover, local Serbs and Montenegrins continued to be overrepresented in the administration, party, and governmental bodies; held better-paid jobs; and enjoyed a higher standard of living than the Albanians.

In many respects, Kosovë was Yugoslavia's "Third World." Its underdevelopment was explained, in part, as a legacy of the extreme backwardness it inherited. The main reason for its continued lagging behind, however, was lack of sufficient investments. During the period from 1945 to 1981, the total per capita investments in Kosovë amounted to only 50 percent of the average of the country as a whole.[57] It was only in the late 1960s and in the 1970s that Kosovë received special treatment and was granted substantial assistance. Nevertheless, the volume of investment was below the Yugoslav average. During the mid-1970s, Kosovë's investments increased at an annual rate of 6.2 percent, which was 43 percent less than the country as a whole and 76 percent below what had been planned. By 1979 per capita annual income in the province had fallen to 27.8 percent of the Yugoslav average.[58]

With the steady deterioration of the economy and growing discontent and unrest among Albanians, Kosovë experienced the emergence of a movement for a separate republic encompassing all the Albanians in Yugoslavia. It attracted a coalition of various people—students, academics, journalists, workers, farmers, and party members—with potentially political significance. Students and intellectuals, who were born and raised in Tito's Yugoslavia, became the staunchest proponents of an Albanian republic. Frustrated by political, economic, and ethnic discrimination, they directed their activities toward breaking Serbia's clamp on Kosovë. They tried to persuade other Yugoslav ethnic groups that establishing an Albanian republic was possible and desirable. Such a step, they argued, would strengthen rather than weaken the federation. The underground press articulated the issue for Albanian political autonomy, analyzed the socioeconomic and political problems facing Kosovë, denounced the persecution of ethnic Albanians, and suggested alternatives to the current political and territorial arrangements.

KOSOVË IN THE 1980s

With the rise of popular discontent and underground activities in the Albanian-inhabited areas, Belgrade could not have failed to anticipate how broadly based the support of ethnic Albanians for a republic would be. The central authorities, however, showed ineptitude and insensitivity toward Kosovar demands. They even refused to recognize publicly that a problem existed, insisting that the issue of ethnic Albanians had been "solved." The YLC had failed to take the initiative and attempt to shape Albanian demands along less confrontational lines. No possibility was provided for regulating conflict through established party and government institutions. Nor did the opportunity exist for a peaceful expression of ethnic Albanians' grievances.

It was against the backdrop of Belgrade's inflexibility and insensitivity that Kosovë exploded in the spring of 1981. What began as a student demonstration at Kosovë University on March 11 had developed into a full-scale popular uprising by the beginning of April. In what was apparently the most striking mass protest against Yugoslavia's Communist regime since 1945, tens of thousands of Albanians took to the streets demanding the improvement of Kosovë's economic conditions, freedom of the press, equal rights with other ethnic groups, release of political prisoners, and republican status for Kosovë. There were reportedly also demands for a union with Albania.

Belgrade refused to grant Kosovë republican status that had the potential of long-term stability. Instead, the uprising was crushed in a manner that disregarded any respect for Albanians' most fundamental national and human rights. The army, police, and militia used tanks to restore order. A curfew was imposed, public gatherings were banned, the university was shut down, and a state of emergency was proclaimed. Thousands of people were arrested. A widespread purge resulted in the replacement of the entire provincial leadership, including Bakalli, and of many cadres at all levels of Kosovar society. A Belgrade-sponsored media campaign was launched against the Albanians, with public attacks made against their history, culture, and heritage. Official and media reports of Albanian demonstrations were characterized by fundamental distortions. The nature of Albanian demands was misrepresented; the socioeconomic causes of the uprising were minimized and vaguely defined domestic and foreign "enemies" blamed. Albanians' subordinate position in the federation and their repression were largely ignored. Albanian nationalists were accused of attempting to create an "ethnically pure" Kosovë, which eventually would be incorporated into a "Greater Albania." Bakalli and his closest associates came under harsh criticism for allegedly having underestimated the danger of Albanian nationalism, for having failed to establish a distinction between national affirmation and nationalism, and for having overstepped constitutional principles by loosening links with Serbia and acting in a "federalistic" way, as if Kosovë were in fact a republic.[59]

The position of ethnic Albanians rapidly deteriorated. Large segments of the population were affected—directly or indirectly—by the government's repression. In an attempt to extinguish Albanian identity, the authorities, in the words of a senior Serbian official, declared war on the "Albanian national consciousness."[60] Such issues as education in the Albanian language, Albanian textbooks, development of cultural programs, and the display of the Albanian flag and other ethnic symbols became subjects of dispute. The main target of criticism became, once again, the Albanian intelligentsia; Kosovë University was described as "a fortress of Albanian nationalism."

Throughout the 1980s, rising ethnic tensions in the Albanian-inhabited territories were characterized by escalating provocations against the Kosovars. Under strong Serbian pressure, Kosovar authorities were forced to change the Albanian flag. In an attempt to suppress Albanian nationalist activity, the government also used measures clearly in violation of the country's constitution and alien to modern legal systems. The concept of collective responsibility was widely used against family members and close relatives of imprisoned Albanians, resulting in the persecution of many innocent people.

The Kosovë problem assumed a new and potentially dangerous dimension in early 1986 with large-scale Serbian demonstrations in Kosovë and calls by prominent Serbian officials, religious leaders, and intellectuals for the introduction of emergency measures in the province. At these gatherings Serbian activists and Communist officials insisted that the problem could only be solved by declaring a state emergency and eliminating the province's autonomy altogether, and they accused Albanians of carrying out "genocide" against local Serbs and Monte-negrins. Serbian and Montenegrin gatherings spread to Serbia, Mon-tenegro, and Vojvodina, eventually causing the downfall of the Vojvodina leadership.

The issue of population growth among the Albanians was also politicized. In 1988 Kosovë's population growth was 73 percent higher than that of Serbia and 30 percent higher than the Yugoslav average. A study by the Belgrade Demographic Research Center concluded that if Kosovë's population continued to grow at the 1988 rate it would double in thirty-two years, reaching 3.5 million inhabitants.[61] The authorities proposed administrative measures to stem the rising population rate among Albanians. Macedonia approved a policy aimed at limiting the number of children per Albanian couple to two. This policy was to be implemented not through persuasion and education but through harsh administrative measures. Nevertheless, it had little chance of success. Traditional Albanian practices tended to encourage large families. Hard economic realities may have been more instrumental in limiting family size, at least in the urban areas, than any population plan. Economic austerity and belt-tightening became the order of the day, and parents simply had to acknowledge that they could no longer afford to raise many children.

Nevertheless, Albanians in general viewed the implementation of family planning policies as highly discriminatory. During a Kosovë Assembly session in December 1988, an Albanian delegate wondered why Albanians were discriminated against, because a higher birthrate was "stimulated in other areas" but "administratively prohibited" in Kosovë. Another delegate inquired "whether a law on the restriction of births existed anywhere in the world, and whether things that are being done in Kosovë existed anywhere in the world."[62] The Albanian intelligentsia also denounced forced family planning. Rexhep Qosja, former director of the Institute of Albanological Studies and one of Kosovë's preeminent literary scholars, asked, "What kind of political and intellectual morality is this, which on the one hand permits the natality of the minority to be limited, while stimulating the natality of the majority to the degree of 'expansion' on the other hand. When has it happened and where, that the living are afraid of the unborn children of their own co-citizens?"[63]

In Macedonia the authorities went much further than in Serbia or Montenegro in their struggle against Albanian "nationalism and separatism." Albanians were forced to use Macedonian names for places, prohibited from giving Albanian "nationalist" names to newborn children, and denied the right to display their national flag. In 1987 the authorities introduced so-called mixed classes in secondary schools, in which instruction was carried out solely in Macedonian. This caused widespread outrage, and demonstrations were organized in 1988 in Kumanovë and Gostivar. Albanians complained that they were being deprived of their constitutional right to education in their mother tongue. The authorities used force to disperse the demonstrations, and many participants received stiff prison sentences. Kosovar intellectuals petitioned Yugoslavia's top state and party leadership, demanding that immediate measures be taken to stop the repression of Albanians in Macedonia.[64]

The migration of Serbs and Montenegrins from Kosovë became one of the most contentious issues in Prishtinë-Belgrade relations. From 1982 to 1986 some 20,000 Serbs and Montenegrins reportedly migrated from Kosovë.[65] Serbian officials and the media maintained that Serbs and Montenegrins were moving out because of pressure and discrimination by the Albanians. Kosovar officials, on the other hand, stressed that the economic situation was the main factor affecting emigration. They supported this argument by pointing out that Albanians, too, were leaving Kosovë in increasing numbers.

In June 1986 Kosovë Assembly adopted a special program in an effort to stop the migration of non-Albanians from the province. Serbs and Montenegrins returning to Kosovë were given priority in employment, housing, and allotment of plots for private houses. The sale of real estate involving Albanians and Serbs was prohibited. Moreover, numerous working groups from both the federal and the republican government were sent to the region, which prompted a prominent Albanian official, Ismail Bajra, to complain that Kosovë's legal institutions were being suspended.[66] During 1987 alone some 600 activists and Serbian party Central Committee members were sent to Kosovë,[67] bypassing provincial legal institutions.

With Slobodan Milošević's rise to power in Serbia and in conjunction with the repressive campaign against Kosovar activists and the intelligentsia, a well-coordinated campaign was launched against Kosovë's political elite. The older generation of leaders—such as Fadil Hoxha, Xhavit Nimani, Imer Pula, and Xhevdet Hamza—who had led the partisan movement and had served Yugoslavia well for over four decades, were expelled from the party. Fadil Hoxha, who at one time had served as Yugoslavia's vice-president, was blamed by a special commission of the Yugoslav party's Central Committee for "the policy which led to the escalation of ethnic Albanian chauvinism, separatism and open counterrevolutionary outbursts in 1968 and 1981." Significantly, the downfall of Hoxha did not result in popular disturbances. This reflected the widespread disappointment with his stand after the 1981 demonstrations, when Hoxha made several public speeches sharply attacking Albanian demonstrators.[68] Many Kosovars apparently never forgave Hoxha for his failure to side with his own people at the most critical moments in the post–World War II history of Kosovë, such as during Ranković's rule and the 1968 and 1981 demonstrations. A dangerous gap had divided the masses from the elites, who were the major beneficiaries of the post-Ranković era transformations. If Belgrade now blamed Fadil Hoxha and his closest associates for the deterioration of ethnic relations in Kosovë, Albanian masses considered them Serbian "surrogates." Young officials with "a Yugoslav view of the future of the country,"[69] were appointed to leading positions in the province, the most prominent of them being Azem Vllasi, who was named Kosovë party leader in 1986. But to Serbia's disappointment, the younger generation of leaders turned out to be as determined as their predecessors in defending the province's autonomy.

In fall 1988 Milošević intensified the campaign to bring Kosovë under Serbia's total control. Through the manipulation of mass street gatherings of Serbs and Montenegrins and various pressures, Milošević pushed for constitutional changes to "enable Serbia to constitute itself as a republic." He appeared determined that Serbia's legislative authority be extended to cover most important spheres of life in Kosovë and Vojvodina. Vllasi, who had opposed Milošević's campaign to restrict Kosovë's autonomy, was dismissed from the provincial leadership and eventually expelled from the Yugoslav party Central Committee. He had become highly popular among the Albanians, and his ouster prompted widespread demonstrations in November 1988 and worker protests in early 1989.[70]

What propelled the cycle of unrest in Kosovë was Milošević's determination to deny the Albanians even the limited political and cultural autonomy they enjoyed according to the country's 1974 constitution, even at the risk of turning Yugoslavia into another Lebanon. Belgrade insisted that Albanian nationalism was undermining the country's stability and was fed by foreign forces, namely, Tiranë and Albanian communities in the West. But there was no mention of the negative impact of the Yugoslav army and security forces' excesses in Albanian regions or the widespread anti-Albanian sentiments that fueled the conflict. Albanian moderate leaders, such as Vllasi, were outflanked, on the one hand, by leaders coopted by Belgrade who supposedly thought in a "Yugoslav way" but enjoyed little support among the masses and, on the other, by an increasing number of people who had given up hope that Kosovë could achieve full political autonomy by working within the system and operated through illegal groups and organizations.

Meanwhile, the Albanian intelligentsia, which in the wake of the 1981 unrest had adopted a passive stand, by the late 1980s emerged as "the real defender" of its nation, sharply denouncing Kosovë's loss of political and cultural autonomy and increasing discrimination against Albanians, especially in Macedonia. In January 1987 a prominent writer, Azem Shkreli, said that in order not to make matters worse Albanian scholars had not responded earlier to the Belgrade-inspired, anti-Albanian media campaign. He added: "A collective mistake has been made, the broad public has been manipulated by a number of semitruths and it will not be easy to compensate for this. Because of all this, I, as an intellectual, do not feel at ease any more in Yugoslavia."[71] Another writer, Ramiz Kelmendi, wondered, "Why is it that we cannot speak 'our own' truth about ourselves like everyone else? Why is it that everyone who attempts to say an honest and sincere word about the situation in Kosovë and about the Albanians is attacked with full fanfare and every available weapon?"[72]

Rexhep Qosja emerged in the forefront of efforts to arrest the further deterioration of the position of the Kosovars. He strongly denounced the discrimination and repression of Albanians and the measures that had been taken to restrict their cultural development. He deplored the lack of academic freedom for Albanian scholars. He also denounced the lack of Prishtinë-Tiranë cultural ties.[73] In April 1988 Serbian writers organized a two-day meeting in Belgrade with their Albanian colleagues to discuss relations between the two ethnic groups. Qosja made an impassioned defense of the Albanian cause, speaking out against the "various forms of injustice meted out against the Albanians." The anti-Albanian political campaign being waged in Serbia, Macedonia, and Montenegro, he said, had magnified distrust and intolerance toward Albanians and had created "an anti-Albanian psychosis with dire consequences."[74] The Belgrade meeting was characterized by such contentious discussions that the provincial leadership cancelled the second meeting, scheduled to be held in Prishtinë.

Qosja's advocacy of humanism and condemnation of discrimination and assimilation of Albanians earned him the enmity of Serbia's leaders and writers. But among Albanians he was highly respected and came to be regarded as the most courageous member of Kosovë's post–World War II cultural elite. He did not see himself as a dissident and insisted he was loyal to Yugoslavia. But he contended that the treatment of Albanians, especially in Macedonia, was not only anticonstitutional but bordered on racism. He seemed to offend the government because he relied on Communist party pronouncements on "brotherhood and unity." In an interview in a Croatian magazine in March 1988, Qosja said:

> It is obvious, unfortunately, that in certain communities the Albanians are persistently viewed as members of a minority whose duty it is just to listen and do what they are told without thinking. It is forgotten that people's equality is based not only on the facts of economic and social life, but also on the fact of free use of political intelligence. Humility has always borne the imprint of second-class and third-class citizens. But we proclaim ourselves to be a society of equal citizens and nationalities. Let us be so not only in resolutions, but also in practice.[75]

Despite the continuing crackdown, the suppression of Albanian nationalist pressures for greater autonomy not only intensified those sentiments but aggravated an already turbulent situation. A Belgrade newspaper reported in March 1988 that imprisonment, far from failing to change the attitudes of the majority of Kosovar prisoners, had "actually strengthened their determination."[76] As a result of the Serbian backlash, Albanians' alienation from the rest of Yugoslavia had become more widespread. The Kosovar majority was protective of the so-called nationalists and irredentists and was likely to remain so. In spite of the state of emergency and the stationing of large army and special police units, the unrest spread. The opening of the trial against Vllasi and 14 other prominent Kosovars in October 1989 was followed by almost daily street demonstrations. Taking advantage of the democratization process in the rest of Yugoslavia, Kosovars created several alternative organizations advocating a Western style democratic system. The most important organization was the Democratic League of Kosovë, formed in December 1989 and led by the writer Ibrahim Rugova. Three months after its creation, the Democratic League of Kosovë claimed it had more than 300,000 members. The Communist party had lost all credibility and will probably be defeated in any free election.

On January 23 and 24, 1990, tens of thousands of Albanians staged peaceful demonstrations in Prishtinë, demanding parliamentary democracy, the release of all political prisoners, and an end to political trials. Instead of opening a dialogue, the authorities used force to disperse the demonstrators. The result was predictable: For the next month, thousands of Albanians battled special police forces all over the province. According to official reports, at least 34 people were killed and hundreds injured. The Democratic League of Kosovë issued a statement calling for a dialogue:

> Democratic dialogue is a general demand in Kosovë and the only way to objectively analyze and solve Kosovë's problems. We invite all those active in political life in Kosovë, all alternative currents and groups, the relevant provincial authorities, and all other interested persons to an open, equal, and unconditional dialogue, without preconditions and other restrictions, on current issues concerning the present state of Kosovë and its further development.[77]

Serbia's leaders rejected the call, terming the demonstrators as "terrorists and separatists."

CONCLUSION

To the younger generation of Albanians, the post-1945 political arrangements made little sense. They pushed for reforms that would upgrade their status as citizens of Yugoslavia and as a distinct ethnic entity. The numbers alone provided a graphic example of the enormity of the Kosovë problem. By 1990, Albanians had become the third largest ethnic group in Yugoslavia. But the status and recognition accorded the Albanians were not commensurate with their number and publicly voiced preferences. Their calls for a republic within Yugoslavia represented neither an unrealistic nor an extreme demand. Albanians displayed all the distinctive features necessary for the creation of their own republic. Compact Albanian-inhabited territories included not only Kosovë, where Albanians accounted for 90 percent of the population, but also territories in Montenegro and Macedonia. The Albanians were distinguishable from other ethnic groups not only by their language but also by other social and cultural characteristics. They outnumbered the Montenegrins, Macedonians, and Slovenes, all of whom had their own republics, yet Kosovë remained an integral part of Serbia, the Albanians dispersed among different administrative units. For most Albanians, Belgrade's reasons for denying them the status of a republic had lost whatever plausibility they may have had and boiled down to the issue of whether a non-Slav nationality could ever attain full political equality in the homeland of the South Slavs. Whereas no senior Yugoslav official has addressed this central issue, Belgrade must sooner or later come to grips with it. A realistic policy requires Serbia to eschew the idea of treating the province as a colony and Albanians as second-class citizens. For Serbs, Kosovë entails a choice between bad and worse options: granting the province the status of a separate republic or continued unrest with prospects of violent confrontation and bloodshed.

Serbian leaders, particularly Milošević, showed a remarkable ignorance of the lesson of Ranković's policies. The heavy-handed treatment of Albanians during the 1980s produced explosive resentment. Rather than contain Albanian nationalism, repression served mainly to consolidate it by reinforcing traditional bonds among Kosovars and intensifying their ethnic consciousness. The majority of Albanians continued to nurse a deep sense of injury against the government, but more specifically against Serbia and Serbs everywhere. Cleavages between the two ethnic groups had never been deeper. Good reason existed for concern that the policy of keeping Kosovë under Serbian control could lead to periodic disturbances and protests and, if pursued over a long period of time, eventually to violent confrontation, the introduction of martial law, and armed uprising.

The ethnic conflict in Kosovë is likely to be prolonged. The Yugoslav government, unable to formulate a comprehensive plan for the ultimate resolution of the problem, persisted in pursuing policies that had patently failed after the 1981 events. Whereas in the 1980s Kosovë conflict threatened neither the regime nor the country's territorial integrity, Yugoslavia seemed to be reaching the point where a stable political accommodation between Albanians and Serbs was becoming increasingly difficult, with unthinkable consequences for both sides. Throughout the post-1945 period, most Albanian activists had maintained that Kosovars should rely on legal means alone to obtain their objectives of full political autonomy within the Yugoslav federation. The idea of union with Albania was seriously promoted by very few activists, even in 1990. But the possibility cannot be ruled out that the nature of the Albanian question could change from demands for greater autonomy to demands for secession, especially should the situation in Albania change for the better. With Belgrade's malevolent intransigence, increasing repression, and the loss of political and cultural autonomy, Albanians had little stake in Yugoslavia. Serbian leaders will have no one to blame but themselves if in the future Yugoslavia is confronted with an Albanian *intifada*.

Notes

Notes to Chapter One

1. The Academy of Sciences of the PSR of Albania, *Fjalori Enciklopedik Shqiptar* [The Albanian Encyclopedic Dictionary], (Tiranë, 1985), pp. 1038–41.

2. Androkli Kostallari, "The Contemporary Albanian Diaspora and the Standard National Literary Language," *Studime Filologjike* 3 (1986), p. 21.

3. *Zëri i Popullit*, July 9, 1989.

4. Ibid., June 21, 1989.

5. Ibid., July 9, 1989.

6. *Tanjug Domestic Service in Serbo-Croatian*, 0148 GMT, January 3, 1988, trans. in Foreign Broadcast Information Service, *Daily Report: Eastern Europe* (Washington, D.C.—hereafter FBIS-EEU), 88-003, January 6, 1988, p. 58.

7. Hivzi Islami, "The Belated Demographic Transition in Kosovë in the Framework of the Transitional Demographic Period in Yugoslavia and Europe," *Sociologija* 3 (July–September 1985), pp. 361–77.

8. *Rilindja* (Prishtinë), November 22, 1987.

9. Stavro Skendi, ed., *Albania* (New York: Praeger, 1956), p. 16.

Notes to Chapter Two

1. Ramiz Alia, *Fjalime e Biseda, 1985* [Speeches and Conversations, 1985], vol. 1 (Tiranë: "8 Nëntori," 1986), pp. 20–32.

2. Ramadan Marmullaku, *Albania and the Albanians* (Hamden, Conn.: Archon Books, 1975), pp. 66–67, 71.

3. Peter R. Prifti, *Socialist Albania Since 1944: Domestic and Foreign Developments* (Cambridge, Mass.: MIT Press, 1978), p. 33.

4. According to Anton Logoreci, Hoxha operated "in a situation in which no recognizable sanctions of any kind—moral, ethical, religious, political or judicial—were allowed to function. Following the example of his master Stalin, his own embodiment of the party's will became the supreme law of the land, an absolute *raison d'état*. All moral and human values, including the code of personal honor and fidelity which lay at the heart of the ethics of Albania's peasant society, were contemptuously swept aside to make room for the dogma

of infallibility of the communist party and of its leader." Anton Logoreci, *The Albanians: Europe's Forgotten Survivors* (Boulder, Colo.: Westview Press, 1978), p. 200.

5. Jon Halliday, ed., *The Artful Albanian: The Memoirs of Enver Hoxha* (London: Chatto and Windus, 1986), p. 16.

6. Sulo Gradeci, *30 vjet pranë shokut Enver: Kujtime* [Thirty Years With Comrade Enver: Memoirs] (Tiranë: "8 Nëntori," 1986).

7. Enver Hoxha, *Vite të vegjëlisë* [Years of Childhood] (Tiranë: "8 Nëntori," 1983), pp. 77–90.

8. Enver Hoxha, *Vite të rinisë* [Years of Youth] (Tiranë: "8 Nëntori," 1988).

9. Marmullaku, *Albania and the Albanians*, p. 67.

10. For an official account of Albania's pre–World War II communist movement, see Institute of Marxist-Leninist Studies at the Central Committee of the APL, *Historia e Partisë së Punës të Shqipërisë* [The History of the Albanian Party of Labor], 2d ed. (Tiranë: "8 Nëntori," 1981), pp. 11–74. See also Nicholas C. Pano, *The People's Republic of Albania* (Baltimore, Md.: Johns Hopkins Press, 1968), pp. 26–43.

11. Ali Hadri, "The Formation of the Communist Party of Albania," *Prilozi za Istoriju Socijalizma* 3 (1966), p. 242; Vladimir Dedijer, *Marrëdhanjet jugosllavo-shqiptare, 1939–1948* [Yugoslav-Albanian Relations, 1939–1948] (Belgrade: Prosveta, 1949), p. 11.

12. Miladin Popović, secretary of the Kosovë regional committee of the Yugoslav Communist Party, played an important role in bringing together the Albanian communist groups. In a report to the Yugoslav party Central Committee, Popović thus described the situation on the eve of the formation of the ACP: "We found disintegration. There were many groups and grouplets (all together eight, among them two Trotskyite). Each of them pulled in its own direction. They often made some 'union' and 'deals' in order to backbite one another in front of us [Yugoslav delegates]. . . . There was enough of everything in those groups, but there was nothing communist." Dedijer, *Marrëdhanjet jugosllavo-shqiptare*, p. 15.

13. *Historia e Partisë së Punës të Shqipërisë*, pp. 204–05.

14. Dedijer, *Marrëdhanjet jugosllavo-shqiptare*, p. 146.

15. Milovan Djilas, *Conversations With Stalin* (New York: Harcourt, Brace and World, 1962), p. 144.

16. Pano, *The People's Republic of Albania*, p. 116.

17. Enver Hoxha, *Raport "Mbi aktivitetin e keshillit të përgjithshëm dhe detyrat e mëtejshme të Frontit Demokratik"* [Report "On the Activities of the General Council and the Future Tasks of the Democratic Front"] (Tiranë, 1955), pp. 49–51; and Paul Lendvai, *Eagles in Cobwebs: Nationalism and Communism in the Balkans* (New York: Doubleday, 1969), p. 236.

18. Nicholas C. Pano, "Albania: The Last Bastion of Stalinism," in Milorad M. Drachkovitch, ed., *East Central Europe: Yesterday, Today, Tomorrow* (Stanford, Calif.: Hoover Institution Press, 1982), p. 198.

19. For a more general analysis of the Tiranë-Beijing alliance see Elez Biberaj, *Albania and China: A Study of an Unequal Alliance* (Boulder, Colo.: Westview Press, 1986).

20. For a detailed analysis of the Albanian Cultural Revolution see Nicholas C. Pano, "The Albanian Cultural Revolution," *Problems of Communism* 23, no. 4 (July–August 1974), pp. 44–57.

21. Enver Hoxha, *Report Submitted to the 6th Congress of the APL* (Tiranë: "Naim Frashëri," 1976), p. 19. See also Hoxha's *Reflections on China*, 2 vols. (Tiranë: "8 Nëntori," 1979), and *Imperialism and the Revolution* (Tiranë: "8 Nëntori," 1979).

22. According to Gradeci, in October 1973 Hoxha suffered his first of several heart attacks. Gradeci, *30 vjet pranë shokut Enver*, pp. 397–99.

23. *Kushtetuta e Republikës Popullore Socialiste të Shqipërisë* [The Constitution of the People's Socialist Republic of Albania] (Tiranë, 1976), Article 28.

24. Enver Hoxha, *Report Submitted to the 7th Congress of the APL* (Tiranë: "8 Nëntori," 1976), pp. 166, 200.

25. "On China's Forced Cessation of Aid to Albania," *Peking Review*, July 21, 1978, p. 23.

26. Enver Hoxha, *Albania is Forging Ahead Confidently and Unafraid* (Tiranë: "8 Nëntori," 1978), p. 20.

27. Bardhyl Golemi and Vladimir Misja, *Zhvillimi i arsimit të lartë në Shqipëri* [The Development of Higher Education in Albania] (Tiranë: "8 Nëntori," 1987), p. 172.

Notes to Chapter Three

1. Quoted in Paul Lendvai, *Eagles in Cobwebs: Nationalism and Communism in the Balkans* (New York: Doubleday, 1969), p. 238. In his memoirs, former Soviet leader Nikita S. Khrushchev claimed that President Tito of Yugoslavia told him that Shehu "personally strangled" Minister of Internal Affairs Koçi Xoxe after the Albanian-Yugoslav break in 1948. Strobe Talbott, ed., *Khrushchev Remembers* (Boston: Little, Brown, 1970), p. 476.

2. Sulo Gradeci, *30 vjet pranë shokut Enver: Kujtime* [Thirty Years With Comrade Enver: Memoirs] (Tiranë: "8 Nëntori," 1986), p. 399.

3. Ibid., p. 410.

4. Hoxha's most important publications in this series, all published by "8 Nëntori," were *Imperialism and the Revolution* (1978); *Yugoslav "Self-Administration"—A Capitalist Theory and Practice* (1978); *Reflections on China*, 2 vols. (1979); *The Khrushchevites* (1980); and *The Titoites* (1982).

5. *Bashkimi*, April 27, 1980.

6. Enver Hoxha, *Raporte e Fjalime, 1982–1983* [Reports and Speeches, 1982–1983] (Tiranë: "8 Nëntori," 1985), p. 12.

7. Ibid., pp. 53, 176, 210–11, and 375.

8. Mehmet Shehu, *Vepra të zgjedhura* [Selected Works], vol. 1 (Tiranë: "8 Nëntori," 1981), pp. v–viii.

9. *Zëri i Popullit*, May 30, 1981.

10. *Albanian Telegraphic Agency News Bulletin*, April 28–30, 1985, p. 8.

11. Gradeci, *30 vjet pranë shokut Enver*, passim.

12. Hoxha claims that Shehu's oldest son, who allegedly was implicated in the plot that his father supposedly had organized, also committed suicide. See Hoxha, *Raporte e Fjalime, 1982–1983*, p. 214.

13. Lleshi apparently was sent into retirement because of his advanced age and was not involved in the Shehu affair.

14. Hoxha, *The Titoites*, pp. 567–633; and *Raporte e Fjalime, 1982–1983*, pp. 184–217.

15. *Corriere della Sera* (Milan), November 4, 1983.

16. Quoted in *The Los Angeles Times*, April 12, 1985.

17. *Zëri i Popullit*, September 16, 1982.

18. The official biography of Alia makes no mention of his having studied in the Soviet Union. The Academy of Sciences of the PSR of Albania, *Fjalori Enciklopedik Shqiptar* [The Albanian Encyclopedic Dictionary] (Tiranë, 1985), pp. 19–20.

19. Ibid.

20. Ramiz Alia, *Stalin and His Work—A Banner of Struggle for all Revolutionaries* (Tiranë: "8 Nëntori," 1979), pp. 6–8, 55–56.

21. Louis Zanga, "Albania Begins the Post-Hoxha Era," RAD Background Report/33 (Eastern Europe), *Radio Free Europe Research*, April 18, 1985, p. 2.

22. In a speech in September 1982, Hoxha referred to Alia as "one of my outstanding cofighters." *Zëri i Popullit*, September 16, 1982. An article published in the same paper shortly before Hoxha's death characterized Alia as "one of Comrade Enver's most distinguished cofighters." Ibid., January 19, 1985.

23. Ibid., April 14, 1985.

24. Enver Hoxha, *Vepra* [Works], vol. 56 (Tiranë: "8 Nëntori," 1987), pp. 470–73.

25. Ramiz Alia, *Fjalime e Biseda, 1986* [Speeches and Conversations, 1986], vol. 2 (Tiranë: "8 Nëntori," 1987), pp. 13, 29.

26. *Zëri i Popullit*, November 4, 1986.

27. ATA in English 0733 GMT, January 14, 1990 in FBIS-EEU-90-016, January 24, 1990, p. 4.

28. *The Independent* (London), March 11, 1989.

29. *Drita*, January 19, 1986.

30. Ibid., February 23, 1986.

31. Ibid., December 15, 1985.

32. *Tiranë Domestic Service in Albanian*, 1430 GMT, March 3, 1988, trans. in FBIS-EEU 88-044, March 7, 1988, pp. 1–5.

33. *Zëri i Popullit*, February 18, 1989.

34. Xhezair Abazi, "For Well-Expressed, Deeply Thought Out and Militant Criticism," *Drita*, June 7, 1987.

35. Neshat Tozaj, *Thikat* [Knives] (Tiranë: "Naim Frashëri," 1989).

36. Ismail Kadare, "'Knives': An Important Novel in the Albanian Literature," *Drita*, October 15, 1989, p. 11.

37. *Drita*, November 19, 1989, pp. 5–6.

38. *Zëri i Popullit*, November 4, 1986.

39. Ibid., August 25, 1987.

40. Ibid., October 9, 1987.

41. Hamit Beqja, "Kindling Further Debate," *Zëri i Popullit*, February 27, 1987.

42. Ibid., October 9 and December 12 and 25, 1986.

43. Ibid., March 17, 1989.

Notes to Chapter Four

1. Amnesty International, *Albania: Political Imprisonment and the Law* (London, 1984). See also Puebla Institute, *Albania: Religion in a Fortress State* (Washington, D.C., 1989).

2. The Minnesota Lawyers International Human Rights Committee, *Human Rights in the People's Socialist Republic of Albania* (Minneapolis, Minn., 1990).

3. Nicholas C. Pano, "Albania: The Last Bastion of Stalinism," in Milorad M. Drachkovitch, ed., *East Central Europe: Yesterday, Today, Tomorrow* (Stanford, Calif.: Hoover Institution Press, 1982), pp. 171–218.

4. See Alia's speech at the 9th Central Committee plenum, *Zëri i Popullitt*, January 25, 1990.

5. Tiranë Domestic Service in Albanian 1900 GMT, February 3, 1990, trans. in FBIS-EEU-90-026, February 7, 1990, pp. 3–8.

6. *The Statute of the Party of Labor of Albania* (Tiranë: "8 Nëntori," 1977).

7. Ramiz Alia, *Fjalime e Biseda, 1986* [Speeches and Conversations, 1986], vol. 2 (Tiranë: "8 Nëntori," 1987), pp. 41–42.

8. *Kongresi i 9-të i Partisë së Punës të Shqipërisë* [The 9th Congress of the Albanian Party of Labor] (Tiranë: "8 Nëntori," 1986), pp. 319–24.

9. *Zëri i Popullit*, November 4, 1986.

10. Ibid., November 2, 1981.

11. Ibid., November 9, 1986.

12. Ibid., February 3, 1989.

13. Ibid., November 4, 1986.

14. Ibid.

15. Ibid., April 24, 1988.

16. Ibid., February 11, 1989.

17. Ibid., February 3, 1987.

18. See Simon Stefani, "The Assurance of the Leading Role of the Party and the Correct Understanding of the Party Directives and of Comrade Enver Hoxha's Teachings—A Guarantee for the Successful Implementation of the Tasks by the Organs of Investigation," *Drejtësia Popullore* 4 (October–December 1983), pp. 3–10; and Sami Gega, "Party Leadership and Control—an Indispensible Objective and the Basis of Every Success," *Rruga e Partisë* 12 (December 1983), pp. 24–33.

19. Ramiz Alia, *Fjalime e Biseda, 1985* [Speeches and Conversations, 1985], vol. 1 (Tiranë: "8 Nëntori," 1986), pp. 66–67. See also Sami Gega, "Intensive and Professional Preventive Work: A Task for the Party and the Specialized Bodies of the Dictatorship of the Proletariat," *Rruga e Partisë* 1 (January 1988), pp. 56–64.

20. *Zëri i Popullit*, September 29, 1989.

21. Ibid., November 4, 1986; Bardhyl Golemi and Vladimir Misja, *Zhvillimi i arsimit të lartë në Shqipëri* [The Development of Higher Education in Albania] (Tiranë, 1987), p. 172; and *Albania: General Information* (Tiranë: "8 Nëntori," 1984), p. 214.

22. Alia, *Fjalime e Biseda, 1985,* vol. 1, pp. 207–210.

23. *Puna,* June 26, 1987.

24. Editorial in *Rruga e Partisë* 3 (March 1984), pp. 10–11.

25. *Neue Züricher Zeitung* (Zürich), June 26, 1985.

26. *Zëri i Popullit,* September 2, 1986.

27. *Zëri i Rinisë,* February 5, 1986.

28. Mehmet Elezi, "Let Us Utilize the Loyalty and Determination of Youth to Progress Always," *Rruga e Partisë* 7 (July 1985), pp. 69–80; and Lisen Bashkurti, "Problems of Upbringing and Civil Behavior Demand Greater Commitment," *Zëri i Rinisë,* August 6, 1988.

29. Hamit Beqja, "The Dialectic of Educating Youth and the Overcoming of Its Contradictions," *Zëri i Popullit,* May 24, 1986.

30. Hamit Beqja, "Against the Taboos That Hamper the Education and Ideological Maturation of Young People," *Zëri i Popullit,* June 17, 1988.

31. *Zëri i Rinisë,* May 28, 1988.

32. Lisen Bashkurti, "Raising the Standards of Conduct and of Young People's Behavior in Society—At the Focus of the Youth Organization's Attention," *Rruga e Partisë* 9 (September 1988), p. 60.

33. *Zëri i Popullit,* September 29, 1989. In her report to the Eighth Plenum, Politburo member, Lenka Çuko, proposed "including more candidates than will be elected on the list for posts in the bureau or posts as secretary and deputy secretary of basic organizations, and the party bureaus in enterprises, agricultural cooperatives, and institutions. Let us elect those who obtain the most votes in secret ballots, but at least 50 percent of the votes. Secretaries and deputy secretaries could be elected directly by the basic organizations." See *Zëri i Popullit,* September 27, 1989.

Notes to Chapter Five

1. For a review of the Albanian economy, see Peter R. Prifti, *Socialist Albania Since 1944: Domestic and Foreign Developments* (Cambridge, Mass.: MIT Press, 1978), pp. 52–89; and Adi Schnytzer, *Stalinist Economic Strategy in Practice: The Case of Albania* (New York: Oxford University Press, 1982).

2. The Academy of Sciences of the PSR of Albania, *Fjalori Enciklopedik Shqiptar* [The Albanian Encyclopedic Dictionary] (Tiranë, 1985), p. 1050.

3. *Zëri i Popullit,* November 22, 1988.

4. Ibid., November 6, 1986.

5. *Ekonomia Popullore* 1 (1973), pp. 37–42.

6. *Kushtetuta e Republikës Popullore Socialiste të Shqipërisë* [The Constitution of the People's Socialist Republic of Albania] (Tiranë, 1976).

7. Albania did not publish full or reliable economic statistical information. Sami Gega, writing in the party's theoretical organ, disclosed that even the statistical information transmitted to the Central Committee was often unreliable.

He said figures given in percentages tended to conceal shortcomings and nonfulfillments of plan targets, giving the leadership a distorted picture of the actual state of affairs. Gega added that "there are some organization secretaries and cadres who do not properly understand the need to inform the communists and the masses about various decisions and directives, or who give out simple information without pausing [to reflect] on its political and ideological content and, even worse, without reflecting on the tasks that emerge for them from these decisions and directives. Some party secretaries try to justify this mistaken attitude with the allegation that they are preserving confidential information which must truly be kept secret, but without determining what constitutes a secret and for whom." See Sami Gega, "The Present Stage of Intensive and Complex Development Requires an Information System that is Rapid, Concrete, Objective and Capable of Treating Problems," *Rruga e Partisë* 6 (June 1986), p. 50.

8. *Zëri i Popullit*, April 9, 1986.

9. Ibid., November 4, 1986.

10. Ibid., November 10, 1986.

11. Ibid., December 28, 1988.

12. Ibid., December 28, 1989.

13. Alia speech at the Vlorë district party plenum, *Tiranë Domestic Service in Albanian*, 1900 GMT, March 22, 1988, trans. in FBIS-EEU-88-057, March 24, 1988, pp. 2–6.

14. Alia speech at Librazhd party *aktiv*, *Zëri i Popullit*, September 25, 1987.

15. *Zëri i Popullit*, October 30, 1987.

16. Ibid., August 27, 1987.

17. During 1983 alone, 770,000 working days were lost, the equivalent of the daily absence of 2,500 workers. In the first six months of 1984, absenteeism resulted in a loss of 340,000 workdays, the equivalent of an absenteeism from work of 2,200 laborers daily. During a similar period in 1985, some 235,000 workdays, the equivalent of the daily absence of 1,500 workers, were lost. See *Zëri i Popullit*, September 9, 1984, and August 26, 1985.

18. Ibid., September 29, 1989.

19. Ibid., September 25, 1987.

20. Ibid., May 13, 1988.

21. Ramiz Alia, *Fjalime e Biseda, 1986* [Speeches and Conversations, 1986], vol. 2 (Tiranë: "8 Nëntori," 1987), pp. 167–68.

22. Pirro Kondi (first secretary of the Tiranë party district), "The Communist—Holder and Dispenser of Culture in All Fields of Activity," *Zëri i Popullit*, August 6, 1988, p. 2.

23. Enver Hoxha, *Raporte e Fjalime, 1982–1983* [Reports and Speeches, 1982–1983] (Tiranë: "8 Nëntori," 1985), p. 53.

24. Vjollca Kallajxhi, "For the Development of Trade in Harmony with the Ever-Increasing Demands of the Population," *Rruga e Partisë* 2 (February 1983), pp. 22–29; and Osman Murati, "Supplying the People in a Continually Improved Manner with Consumer Goods Requires the Strengthening of Organizational Work in Trade Organs," *Rruga e Partisë* 7 (July 1984), pp. 28–37.

25. *Zëri i Popullit*, September 12, 1985.

26. Ibid., March 12, 1987.

27. Ramiz Alia, *Fjalime e Biseda, 1987* [Speeches and Conversations, 1987], vol. 4 (Tiranë: "8 Nëntori," 1988), p. 317.

28. Alia, *Fjalime e Biseda, 1986*, vol. 3, pp. 63–64.

29. *Zëri i Popullit*, February 13, 1987; and *Bashkimi*, March 12, 1987.

30. *Zëri i Popullit*, November 4, 1986.

31. Alia, *Fjalime e Biseda, 1986*, vol. 3, p. 427.

32. Sabah Hilmia, "Let Us Further Refine the Use of Certain Economic Factors of Socialism," *Rruga e Partisë* 7 (July 1986), pp. 48–50.

33. Robert Koli, "Responding Better to Purchasing Power—A Direct Expression of the People's Increasing Prosperity," *Rruga e Partisë* 8 (August 1988), p. 27.

34. *Bashkimi*, October 2, 1988.

35. *Zëri i Popullit*, June 12, 1988.

36. Bardhyl Ceku and Astrit Avdyli, "For a Better Fulfillment of the Real Needs of the Population for Consumer Commodities," *Rruga e Partisë* 11 (November 1988), pp. 29–38.

37. Gëzim Koni, "Improving the Supply of the People Demands Constant and Coordinated Efforts," *Rruga e Partisë* 9 (September 1987), pp. 5–13.

38. Editorial in *Zëri i Popullit*, June 16, 1988.

39. *Zëri i Popullit*, November 10, 1988.

40. Ibid., December 14, 1988.

41. Alia, *Fjalime e Biseda, 1987*, vol. 4, p. 107.

42. Koli, "Responding Better to Purchasing Power," pp. 22–27.

43. *Zëri i Popullit*, May 7, 1988.

44. Ibid., February 5, 1989.

45. Ibid., February 3, 1989.

46. Ibid., February 5, 1989.

47. Ibid., November 4, 1986.

48. Alia, *Fjalime e Biseda, 1987*, vol. 4, pp. 11–12, 292.

49. Ibid., pp. 366–67.

50. Ibid., pp. 309–10.

51. *Rruga e Partisë* 4 (April 1987), pp. 12–13.

52. *Zëri i Popullit*, March 21, 1987.

53. Ibid., April 11, 1987.

54. Foto Çami, "Our Science Should Competently Confront the Great Tasks Set Out by the 9th APL Congress," *Rruga e Partisë* 4 (April 1987), p. 12.

55. *Zëri i Popullit*, October 9, 1987.

56. Alia, *Fjalime e Biseda, 1986*, vol. 3, pp. 246–47.

Notes to Chapter Six

1. Julian Birch, "Albania—the Reluctant Puppet," *Journal of Social and Political Studies* 2 (Winter 1977), p. 291.

2. Enver Hoxha, *Raporte e Fjalime, 1982–1983* [Reports and Speeches, 1982–1983] (Tiranë: "8 Nëntori," 1985), p. 375.

3. Ramiz Alia, *Politikë në shërbim të socializmit, lirisë dhe pavarësisë së atdheut* [A Policy in the Service of Socialism, Freedom, and Independence of the Motherland] (Tiranë: "8 Nëntori," 1983), pp. 15–18.

4. *Zëri i Popullit*, November 28, 1984.

5. *Business Eastern Europe*, March 30, 1984, p. 98.

6. Ibid., December 16, 1983, p. 400, and February 3, 1984, p. 34.

7. *ANSA in English*, December 21, 1984.

8. *Zëri i Popullit*, November 28, 1984. See also Enver Hoxha, *Dy popuj miq* [Two Friendly Peoples] (Tiranë: "8 Nëntori," 1985), pp. 421–22.

9. Committee on Foreign Affairs, U.S. House of Representatives, *U.S. Policy Toward Eastern Europe, 1985* (Washington, D.C.: U.S. Government Printing Office, 1986), p. 6.

10. *Pravda*, November 29, 1986.

11. Ramiz Alia, *Fjalime e Biseda, 1986* [Speeches and Conversations, 1986], vol. 3 (Tiranë: "8 Nëntori," 1987), p. 56.

12. *Zëri i Popullit*, September 10, 1985.

13. Ibid., November 8, 1986.

14. Foto Çami, "A Great Marxist-Leninist Theoretician and Revolutionary," in *Konferencë kombëtare kushtuar veprës së pavdekshme të shokut Enver Hoxha* [National Conference Dedicated to the Immortal Work of Comrade Enver Hoxha] (Tiranë: "8 Nëntori," 1985), p. 37.

15. Muhamet Kapllani, "Inspirer, Architect, and Implementor of the Strategy and Tactics of Our Foreign Policy of Proletarian Principles," *Rruga e Partisë* 6 (June 1985), p. 18.

16. Hoxha, *Dy popuj miq*, p. 413.

17. *Zëri i Popullit*, October 9, 1987.

18. Ibid., July 12, 1987.

19. Ibid., November 29, 1987.

20. Ibid., July 12, 1987.

21. Ibid., September 29, 1987.

22. *Tanjug in English*, 1201 GMT, February 19, 1988, in FBIS-EEU 88-035, February 23, 1988, p. 21.

23. Interview with Yugoslav Deputy Foreign Minister Milivoje Maksić, *Avanti* (Rome), March 5, 1988, trans. in FBIS-EEU 88-052, March 17, 1988, pp. 43–45.

24. *Zëri i Popullit*, February 25, 1988.

25. Ibid., January 21, 1989.

26. For a more detailed review of Albanian-Yugoslav relations see Elez Biberaj, "Albanian-Yugoslav Relations and the Question of Kosovë," *East European Quarterly* 16, no. 4 (January 1983), pp. 485–510; Patrick F. R. Artisien, *Friends or Foes? Yugoslav-Albanian Relations over the last 40 Years* (Bradford, England: University of Bradford Postgraduate School of Yugoslav Studies, 1980); Enver Hoxha, *The Titoites: Historical Notes* (Tiranë: "8 Nëntori," 1982); Vladimir Dedijer, *Marrëdhanjet jugosllavo-shqiptare, 1939–1948* [Yugoslav-Albanian Relations, 1939–1948] (Belgrade: Prosveta, 1949); and *Relationship Between Yugoslavia and Albania* (Belgrade: Review of International Affairs, 1984).

27. *Zëri i Popullit,* November 4, 1986.

28. Ibid., January 29, 1987.

29. Ibid., February 26, 1988.

30. Quoted in *Zëri i Popullit,* March 5, 1987.

31. *Tanjug in English,* 0929 GMT, May 13, 1988, in FBIS-EEU 88-097, May 19, 1988, p. 57. In 1986 some 10,000 Yugoslavs reportedly visited Albania. *Politika* (Belgrade), March 10, 1987, p. 7, trans. in FBIS-EEU, March 26, 1987, p. I/10.

32. *Tanjug Domestic Service in Serbo-Croatian,* 1640 GMT, January 21, 1989, trans. in FBIS-EEU 89-013, January 23, 1989, p. 16.

33. *Albanian Telegraphic Agency in English,* 0920 GMT, February 25, 1989, in FBIS-EEU 89-037, February 27, 1989, p. 2.

34. *Tiranë Domestic Service in Albanian,* 1900 GMT, February 26, 1989, trans. in FBIS-EEU 89-037, February 27, 1989, p. 1.

35. *Tanjug Domestic Service in Serbo-Croatian,* 1511 GMT, March 1, 1989, trans. in FBIS-EEU 89-040, March 2, 1989, pp. 42–45.

36. *Neue Az* (Vienna), February 20, 1987, p. 5, trans. in FBIS-EEU, February 24, 1987, p. I/1; and *Tanjug Domestic Service in Serbo-Croatian,* 0736 GMT, June 29, 1988, trans. in FBIS-EEU 88-135, July 14, 1988, pp. 58–60.

37. Hoxha, *Dy popuj miq,* p. 419.

38. *Athens Domestic Service in Greek,* 1100 GMT, August 28, 1987, trans. in FBIS-EEU, August 31, 1987, p. P/1.

39. *Zëri i Popullit,* November 22, 1987.

40. Ibid., May 16–19, 1985.

41. *AFP in English,* 1442 GMT, September 13, 1985.

42. *DPA in German,* 1438 GMT, October 23, 1987, trans. in FBIS-EEU 87-206, October 26, 1987, p. 2.

43. *Süddeutsche Zeitung* (Munich), November 17, 1987, trans. in FBIS-EEU 87-223, November 19, 1987, p. 4.

44. *DPA in German,* 1527 GMT, November 16, 1987, trans. in FBIS-EEU 87-221, November 17, 1987, p. 1.

45. *DPA in German,* 110 GMT, March 20, 1989, trans. in Foreign Broadcast Information Service, *Daily Report: Western Europe* (Washington, D.C.—hereafter FBIS-WEU), 89-052, March 20, 1989, pp. 8–9.

46. *Jiji in English,* 1441 GMT, March 13, 1989, trans. in FBIS-EEU 89-056, March 24, 1989, p. 13.

47. *Zëri i Popullit,* November 4, 1986.

48. Aristotel Pano, "The Efficiency of Foreign Trade Is Raised Through Comprehensive Efforts, Based on a Real Knowledge of the Situation," *Rruga e Partisë* 8 (August 1987), pp. 34–42.

49. *ADN International Service in German,* 1622 GMT, June 21, 1989, trans. in FBIS-EEU 89-119, June 22, 1989, pp. 5–6.

50. *Zëri i Popullit,* June 20–22, 1989; and ADN International Service in German 1054 GMT, June 20, 1989, trans. in FBIS-EEU 89-118, June 21, 1989, pp. 2–3.

51. *Zëri i Popullit,* December 13, 1989.

52. *Izvestia,* January 28, 1989, trans. in Foreign Broadcast Information Service, *Daily Report: The Soviet Union* (Washington, D.C.—hereafter FBIS-SOV), 89-023, February 6, 1989, pp. 53–54, and March 7, 1989, trans. in FBIS-SOV 89-044, March 8, 1989, p. 43; *Literaturnaya Gazeta,* March 8, 1989, p. 9, trans. in FBIS-SOV 89-046, March 10, 1989, pp. 25–26; and *Sovetskaya Rossiya,* March 30, 1989, p. 3, trans. in FBIS-SOV 89-061, March 31, 1989, pp. 35–36.

Notes to Chapter Seven

1. For a general overview of the Kosovë problem, see Arshi Pipa and Sami Repishti, eds., *Studies on Kosova* (Boulder, Colo.: East European Monographs, 1984); Alex N. Dragnich and Slavko Todorovich, *The Saga of Kosovo: Focus on Serbian-Albanian Relations* (Boulder, Colo.: East European Monographs, 1984); Ramadan Marmullaku, *Albania and the Albanians* (Hamden, Conn.: Archon Books, 1975), pp. 135–52; Peter R. Prifti, *Socialist Albania Since 1944: Domestic and Foreign Developments* (Cambridge, Mass.: MIT Press, 1978), pp. 222–41; Nicholas J. Costa, "Kosovo: A Tragedy in the Making," *East European Quarterly* 21, no. 1 (March 1987), pp. 87–97; Branko Horvat, *Kosovsko Pitanje* [The Kosovë Question] (Zagreb: Globus, 1988); The Academy of Sciences of the PSR of Albania, *The Albanians and Their Territories* (Tiranë: "8 Nëntori," 1985); Hajredin Hoxha, *Afirmimi i kombësisë shqiptare në Jugosllavi* [The Affirmation of the Albanian Nationality in Yugoslavia] (Prishtinë: Rilindja, 1983); and Kurtesh Saliu, *Lindja, zhvillimi, pozita dhe aspektet e autonomitetit të Krahinës Socialiste Autonome të Kosovës në Jugosllavinë Socialiste* [Birth, Development, Position, and Aspects of the Autonomy of the Socialist Autonomous Province of Kosovë in Socialist Yugoslavia] (Prishtinë: Enti i Teksteve dhe i Mjeteve Mësimore, 1984).

2. *Rilindja* (Prishtinë), May 7, 1989.

3. *Borba* (Belgrade), February 23, 1989.

4. *Rilindja,* October 26, 1988.

5. *NIN* (Belgrade), May 10, 1981.

6. *Tanjug Domestic Service in Serbo-Croatian,* 0148 GMT, January 3, 1988, trans. in FBIS-EEU 88-003, January 6, 1988, pp. 57–58.

7. *Jedinstvo* (Prishtinë), February 27, 1986, p. 6, trans. in Joint Publications Research Service, *East Europe Report* (Washington, D.C.—hereafter JPRS-EEU), 86-109, July 24, 1986, pp. 119–20.

8. *Tanjug in English,* 1608 GMT, October 27, 1988, in FBIS-EEU 88-211, November 1, 1988, p. 68.

9. *Rilindja,* January 27, 1989.

10. *Borba,* March 2–3, 1985.

11. *Tanjug in English,* 1935 GMT, November 7, 1988, in FBIS-EEU 88-210, November 10, 1988, pp. 60–61.

12. *Rilindja,* January 21, 1989.

13. Saliu, *Lindja, zhvillimi, pozita,* p. 199.

14. *Jedinstvo,* October 22–25, 1982.

15. *Rilindja,* March 21, 1984.

16. Saliu, *Lindja, zhvillimi, pozita,* p. 199.

17. Ibid., p. 200.

18. *Prishtinë Domestic Service in Albanian*, 1800 GMT, November 2, 1985, trans. in FBIS-EEU, November 12, 1985, p. I/6.

19. *Borba*, July 18, 1986.

20. *Tanjug Domestic Service in Serbo-Croatian*, 1432 GMT, November 11, 1987, trans. in FBIS-EEU 87-219, November 13, 1987, p. 43.

21. Zenun Çelaj, "Say Whatever You Like About Kosovë," *Rilindja*, December 26, 1988, p. 6.

22. *Politika* (Belgrade), November 23, 1988.

23. Ibid., April 8, 1987.

24. Dimitrije Tucoviq, *Sërbia e Shqipëria* [Serbia and Albania] (Prishtinë: Rilindja, 1975), pp. 64–102.

25. Liman Rushiti, *Lëvizja kaçake në Kosovë (1918–1928)* [The Partisan Movement in Kosovë (1918–1928)] (Prishtinë, 1981); and Ajet Haxhiu, *Shota dhe Azem Galica* [Shota and Azem Galica] (Tiranë: "8 Nëntori," 1976).

26. For a useful review of the agrarian reform and its adverse impact on the Kosovars, see Milovan Obradović, *Agrarna reforma i kolonizacija na Kosovu (1918–1941)* [The Agrarian Reform and Colonization of Kosovë (1918–1941)] (Prishtinë, 1981).

27. Hajredin Hoxha, "The Policy of Eliminating Albanians from the Old Yugoslavia," *Përparimi* 5 (1970), p. 432; Hivzi Islami, "Anthropological Research in Kosovë," *Gjurmime Albanologjike: Seria Historike* 1 (1971), pp. 138–44; Ali Hadri, "The Position and Situation of Kosovë in the Yugoslav Kingdom (1918–1941)," *Gjurmime Albanologjike* 2 (1968), pp. 163–91; and Marmullaku, *Albania and the Albanians*, p. 138.

28. Radošin Rajević, "Emergence and Development of the Autonomy of Kosovo within Serbia and Yugoslavia," in *Relationship Between Yugoslavia and Albania* (Belgrade: Review of International Affairs, 1984), pp. 28, 36.

29. Vaso Čubrilović, *The Expulsion of the Albanians*, memorandum presented to the Yugoslav Royal Government, 7 March 1937 (n.d., n.p.), p. 24. See also Hakif Bajrami, "The Suppression and Resistance of the Albanians in Kosovë," *Studime Historike* 2 (1981), pp. 132–34.

30. Hakif Bajrami, *Partia Komuniste e Jugosllavisë në Kosovë, 1919–1941* [The Yugoslav Communist Party in Kosovë, 1919–1941] (Prishtinë, 1982), pp. 195–205; and Paul Lendvai, *Eagles in Cobwebs: Nationalism and Communism in the Balkans* (New York: Doubleday, 1969), p. 225.

31. Asllan Fazlija, *Autonomija e Kosovës e Metohisë në Jugosllavinë Socialiste* [The Autonomy of Kosovë and Metohia in Socialist Yugoslavia] (Prishtinë: Rilindja, 1966), pp. 38–39; and Hajredin Hoxha, "The Process of Self-determination of the Albanian Nationality During the Revolution and the Building of Socialism," *Kosova* 2 (1973), pp. 68–80.

32. Quoted in Rajević, "Emergence and Development," p. 67(n).

33. *E vërteta mbi gjendjen e shqiptarëve në Jugosllavi* [The Truth About the Plight of Albanians in Yugoslavia] (Tiranë, 1960), p. 45; Stanoje Aksić, *Položaj autonomnih pokrajina u ustavnon sistemu SFR Jugoslavije* [The Position of the Autonomous Provinces in the Legal System of the SFR of Yugoslavia] (Belgrade: Naučna Knjiga, 1967), p. 56; and Fazlija, *Autonomija e Kosovës*, p. 39.

34. Aksić, *Položaj autonomnih pokrajina*, p. 56; and Fazlija, *Autonomija e Kosovës*, pp. 39, 46.

35. Enver Hoxha, *With Stalin* (Tiranë: "8 Nëntori," 1979), p. 140; and *Zëri i Popullit*, May 17, 1981.

36. *Zëri i Popullit*, September 9, 1958, and August 31, 1966; Tahir Zajmi, *Lidhja e II e Prizrenit dhe lufta heroike e popullit për mbrojtjen e Kosovës* [The Second Prizren League and the People's Heroic Struggle for the Defense of Kosovë] (Brussels, 1964), pp. 52–88; and Paul Shoup, *Communism and the Yugoslav National Question* (New York: Columbia University Press, 1968), pp. 104–05.

37. *Zëri i Popullit*, September 9, 1959, and August 31, 1966.

38. Abas Ermenji, *Albania* (Paris: National Democratic Committee "Free Albania," 1968), p. 482; and Zajmi, *Lidhja e II e Prizrenit*, p. 55.

39. Rajević, "Emergence and Development," p. 76.

40. Fazlija, *Autonomija e Kosovës*, pp. 78–79.

41. Robert R. King, *Minorities Under Communism: Nationalities as a Source of Tension Among Balkan Communist States* (Cambridge, Mass.: Harvard University Press, 1973), p. 132.

42. Ali Hadri, "The National and Political Development of Albanians in Yugoslavia," in *Klasno i Nacionalno u Suvremenom Socijalizmu* [Class and Nation in Contemporary Socialism] (Zagreb: Naše Teme, 1970), p. 551.

43. See speech by Veli Deva in Šesta Sednica CK SK Srbije, *Aktivnost Saveza Komunista Srbije Posle Četverte Sednice CK SK Jugoslavije* [The Activity of the League of Communists of Serbia After the Fourth Session of the Central Committee of the League of Communists of Yugoslavia] (Belgrade: Sedma Sila, 1966), p. 59.

44. See speech by Xhavit Nimani, *Aktivnost Saveza Komunista*, pp. 248–49; see also Hoxha, *Afirmimi i kombësisë shqiptare*, pp. 76–87.

45. Islami, "Anthropological Research in Kosovë," p. 141.

46. Hadri, "The National and Political Development of Albanians," pp. 540–41.

47. *Borba*, October 14, 1979.

48. Zdenko Antic, "Kosovo's Socioeconomic Development," RAD Background Report/108 (Yugoslavia), *Radio Free Europe Research*, March 23, 1981.

49. Hivzi Islami, "Urbanization and Nationalities in Kosovë," *Përparimi* 4 (1980), pp. 449–50.

50. *Rilindja*, April 3, 1982.

51. *Borba*, April 10, 1968.

52. *Politika*, September 18, 1968; and Belgrade Domestic Service in Serbo-Croatian, 1830 GMT, September 23, 1968, and 1830 GMT, September 30, 1968.

53. Marmullaku, *Albania and the Albanians*, pp. 150–51.

54. Mahmut Bakalli, "The Self-Assertion of the Yugoslav Nationalities Under Self-Management Socialism," *Socialist Thought and Practice* 2 (February 1980), p. 39.

55. Zivko Milić, "A Dossier of the Counterrevolution in Kosovë," *Danas* (Zagreb), April 20, 1982, pp. 80–84.

56. *NIN*, May 10, 1981, p. 21.

57. *Rilindja*, April 9, 1982.

58. *Borba*, July 1, 1979.

59. *Rilindja*, September 26, 1981.

60. Ibid., May 7, 1981.

61. *Tanjug in English*, 1935 GMT, November 7, 1988, in FBIS-EEU 88-218, November 10, 1988, pp. 60–61; and *Tanjug in English*, 1608 GMT, October 27, 1988, in FBIS-EEU 88-211, November 1, 1988, p. 68.

62. Milo Antić, "Giving Birth to Poor Rebels," *Borba*, December 29, 1988, p. 5.

63. Quoted in *Zëri i Popullit*, December 17, 1987, pp. 2–3.

64. *Borba*, November 11, 1988.

65. Ibid., March 5, 1987.

66. *Tanjug Domestic Service in Serbo-Croatian*, 1059 GMT, March 19, 1986, trans. in FBIS-EEU, March 20, 1986, p. I/6–7.

67. *Tanjug Domestic Service in Serbo-Croatian*, 0824 GMT, July 14, 1988, trans. in FBIS-EEU 88-137, July 18, 1988, pp. 56–61.

68. Fadil Hoxha, *Jemi në shtëpinë tonë* [We Are in Our Own Home] (Prishtinë: Rilindja, 1986), vol. 2, pp. 161–205, and vol. 3, pp. 195–245.

69. *Belgrade Domestic Service in Serbo-Croatian*, 0800 GMT, March 30, 1986, trans. in FBIS-EEU, April 1, 1986, pp. I/8–9.

70. See statement by the provincial secretariat for Internal Affairs, *Rilindja*, December 16, 1988; see also ibid., February 5–11, 1989.

71. *Jedinstvo*, January 22, 1987.

72. *Danas*, March 15, 1988, pp. 18–19, trans. in JPRS-EER 88-043, June 3, 1988, pp. 26–29.

73. Quoted in *Zëri i Popullit*, March 5, 1987.

74. *Rilindja*, April 27, 1988.

75. Interview with Rexhep Qosja, "A Gram of Power Weighs More Than a Ton of Intelligence," *Danas*, March 15, 1988, pp. 20–21, trans. in JPRS-EEU 88-043, June 3, 1988, pp. 29–32.

76. *Borba*, March 25, 1988.

77. *Rilindja*, February 1, 1990.

Selected Bibliography

The Academy of Sciences of the PSR of Albania, *The Albanians and Their Territories*. Tiranë: "8 Nëntori," 1985.

––––––. *Fjalori Enciklopedik Shqiptar* [The Albanian Encyclopedic Dictionary]. Tiranë. 1985.

Albania: General Information. Tiranë: "8 Nëntori," 1984.

Alia, Ramiz. *Fjalime e Biseda* [Speeches and Conversations]. 5 vols. Tiranë: "8 Nëntori," 1986–1989.

––––––. *Të populli—forca e jonë* [With the People Lies Our Strength]. Tiranë: "8 Nëntori," 1985.

Amnesty International. *Albania: Political Imprisonment and the Law*. London, 1984.

Artisien, Patrick, F. R. "Albania After Hoxha." *SAIS Review* 6, no. 1 (Winter–Spring 1986), pp. 159–68.

––––––. "Albania at the Crossroads." *The Journal of Communist Studies* 3, no. 3 (September 1987), pp. 231–49.

––––––. "A Note on Kosovo and the Future of Yugoslav-Albanian Relations: A Balkan Perspective." *Soviet Studies* 36, no. 2 (April 1984), pp. 267–76.

Backer, Berit. "Self-Reliance Under Socialism—The Case of Albania." *Journal of Peace Research* 19, no. 4 (1982), pp. 355–67.

Bajrami, Hakif. *Partia Komuniste e Jugosllavisë në Kosovë, 1919–1941* [The Yugoslav Communist Party in Kosovë, 1919–1941]. Prishtinë, 1982.

Biberaj, Elez. *Albania and China: A Study of an Unequal Alliance*. Boulder, Colo.: Westview Press, 1986.

Birch, Julian. "Albania—the Reluctant Puppet." *Journal of Social and Political Studies* 2 (Winter 1977), pp. 269–96.

Brown, J. F. *Eastern Europe and Communist Rule*. Durham, N.C.: Duke University Press, 1988.

––––––. "The Balkans: Soviet Ambitions and Opportunities." *The World Today* 40, no. 6 (June 1984), pp. 244–53.

Costa, Nicholas J. "Albania—A Nation of Contradictions." *East European Quarterly* 22, no. 2 (June 1988), pp. 233–37.

––––––. "Invasion—Action and Reaction: Albania, A Case Study." *East European Quarterly* 10, no. 1 (Spring 1976), pp. 53–63.

————. "Kosovo: A Tragedy in the Making." *East European Quarterly* 21, no. 1 (March 1987), pp. 87–97.

Directory of Statistics, State Planning Commission. *40 Years of Socialist Albania: Statistical Data on the Development of the Economy and Culture*. Tiranë, 1984.

Dragnich, Alex N., and Todorovich, Slavko. *The Saga of Kosovo: Focus on Serbian-Albanian Relations*. Boulder, Colo.: East European Monographs, 1984; distributed by Columbia University Press.

Ermenji, Abas. *Albania*. Paris: National Democratic Committee "Free Albania," 1968.

Gegaj, Athanas, and Krasniqi, Rexhep. *Albania*. New York: Assembly of Captive European Nations, 1964.

Golemi, Bardhyl, and Misja, Vladimir. *Zhvillimi i arsimit të lartë në Shqipëri* [The Development of Higher Education in Albania]. Tiranë: "8 Nëntori," 1987.

Gradeci, Sulo. *30 vjet pranë shokut Enver: Kujtime* [Thirty Years With Comrade Enver: Memoirs]. Tiranë: "8 Nëntori," 1986.

Griffith, William E. *Albania and the Sino-Soviet Rift*. Cambridge, Mass.: MIT Press, 1963.

Halliday, Jon, ed., *The Artful Albanian: The Memoirs of Enver Hoxha*. London: Chatto and Windus, 1986.

Hamm, Harry. *Albania—China's Beachhead in Europe*. New York: Praeger, 1963.

Horvat, Branko. *Kosovsko Pitanje* [The Kosovë Question]. Zagreb: Globus, 1988.

Hoxha, Enver. *Vepra* [Works]. 65 vols. Tiranë: "Naim Frashëri" and "8 Nëntori," 1968–1989.

————. *Vite të vegjëlisë* [Years of Childhood]. Tiranë: "8 Nëntori," 1983.

————. *Vite të rinisë* [Years of Youth]. Tiranë: "8 Nëntori," 1988.

Hoxha, Fadil. *Jemi në shtëpinë tonë* [We Are in Our Own Home]. 3 vols. Prishtinë: Rilindja, 1986.

Hoxha, Hajredin. *Afirmimi i kombësisë shqiptare në Jugosllavi* [The Affirmation of the Albanian Nationality in Yugoslavia]. Prishtinë: Rilindja, 1983.

The Institute of Marxist-Leninist Studies at the Central Committee of the Albanian Party of Labor. *Dokumente Kryesore të Partisë së Punës të Shqipërisë* [Main Documents of the Albanian Party of Labor]. 8 vols. Tiranë: "Naim Frashëri" and "8 Nëntori," 1960–1986.

————. *History of the Party of Labor of Albania*. Tiranë: "Naim Frashëri," 1971.

————. *History of the Party of Labor of Albania, 1966–1980*. Tiranë: "8 Nëntori," 1981.

Islami, Hivzi. *Popullsia e Kosovës: studim demografik* [The Population of Kosovë: A Demographic Study]. Prishtinë, 1981.

Kaser, Michael. "Albania Under and After Enver Hoxha." In Joint Economic Committee, Congress of the United States, *East European Economies: Slow Growth in the 1980s*. Vol. 3, Country Studies on Eastern Europe and Yugoslavia, 1–21. Washington, D.C.: U.S. Government Printing Office, 1986.

————. "Albania's Muscular Socialism." *Contemporary Review* 243 (August 1983), pp. 89–94.

————, and Schnytzer, Adi. "Albania—A Uniquely Socialist Economy." In Joint Economic Committee, Congress of the United States, *East European Econ-*

omies Post-Helsinki, 567–646. Washington, D.C.: U.S. Government Printing Office, 1977.

Keefe, Eugene K., et al. *Area Handbook for Albania.* Washington, D.C.: U.S. Government Printing Office, 1971.

Kessler, Lawrence. "Albania: Performance and Prospects for Trade With the United States and the West." In Joint Economic Committee, Congress of the United States, *East-West Trade: The Prospects to 1985,* 1–21. Washington, D.C.: U.S. Government Printing Office, 1982.

Kolsti, John. "Albania's New Beginning." *Current History* (November 1985), pp. 361–64, 386.

―――. "Albanianism: From the Humanists to Hoxha." In *The Politics of Ethnicity in Eastern Europe,* edited by George Klein and Milan J. Reban, 15–48. Boulder, Colo.: East European Monographs, 1981; distributed by Columbia University Press.

―――. "From Courtyard to Cabinet: The Political Emergence of Albanian Women." In *Women, State, and Party in Eastern Europe,* edited by Sharon L. Wolchik and Alfred G. Meyer, 138–51. Durham, N.C.: Duke University Press, 1985.

Konferencë kombëtare kushtuar veprës së pavdekshme të shokut Enver Hoxha [National Conference Dedicated to the Immortal Work of Comrade Enver Hoxha]. Tiranë: "8 Nëntori," 1985.

Kushtetuta e Republikës Popullore Socialiste të Shqipërisë [The Constitution of the People's Socialist Republic of Albania]. Tiranë, 1976.

Lange, Klaus. "Albanian Marxism's Notion of Revisionism." *Studies in Soviet Thought* 20, no. 1 (July 1979), pp. 61–66.

Larrabee, F. Stephen. "Whither Albania?" *The World Today* 34, no. 2 (February 1978), pp. 61–69.

Logoreci, Anton. *The Albanians: Europe's Forgotten Survivors.* Boulder, Colo.: Westview Press, 1978.

Marmullaku, Ramadan. *Albania and the Albanians.* Hamden, Conn.: Archon Books, 1975.

Misja, Vladimir, Vejsiu, Ylli, and Bërxholi, Arqile. *Popullsia e Shqipërisë* [The Population of Albania]. Tiranë, 1987.

Obradović, Milovan. *Agrarna reforma i kolonizacija na Kosovu (1918–1941)* [The Agrarian Reform and Colonization of Kosovë (1918–1941)]. Prishtinë, 1981.

Pano, Nicholas C. "Albania." In *Communism in Eastern Europe,* 2d ed., edited by Teresa Rakowska-Harmstone, 213–37. Bloomington: Indiana University Press, 1984.

―――. "Albania: The Last Bastion of Stalinism." In *East Central Europe: Yesterday, Today, Tomorrow,* edited by Milorad M. Drachkovitch, 187–218. Stanford, Calif.: Hoover Institution Press, 1982.

―――. *The People's Republic of Albania.* Baltimore, Md.: Johns Hopkins Press, 1968.

Papajorgji, Harilla. *Struktura socialklasore e klasës sonë punëtore* [The Social and Class Composition of Our Working Class]. Tiranë: "8 Nëntori," 1985.

Peters, Stephen. "Ingredients of the Communist Takeover in Albania." *Studies on the Soviet Union* 11, no. 4 (1971), pp. 244–63.

Pipa, Arshi. "Party Ideology and Purges in Albania." *Telos* 59 (Spring 1984), pp. 69–100.

_____, and Repishti, Sami, eds. *Studies on Kosova*. Boulder, Colo.: East European Monographs, 1984; distributed by Columbia University Press.

Pollo, Stefanaq, and Puto, Arben. *The History of Albania*. Boston: Routledge and Kegan Paul, 1981.

Prifti, Peter R. *Socialist Albania Since 1944: Domestic and Foreign Developments*. Cambridge, Mass.: MIT Press, 1978.

Puebla Institute. *Albania: Religion in a Fortress State*. Washington, D.C., 1989.

Relationship Between Yugoslavia and Albania. Belgrade: Review of International Affairs, 1984.

Rushiti, Liman. *Lëvizja kaçake në Kosovë (1918–1928)* [The Partisan Movement in Kosovë (1918–1928)]. Prishtinë, 1981.

Saliu, Kurtesh. *Lindja, zhvillimi, pozita dhe aspektet e autonomitetit të Krahinës Socialiste Autonome të Kosovës në Jugosllavinë Socialiste* [Birth, Development, Position, and Aspects of the Autonomy of the Socialist Autonomous Province of Kosovë in Socialist Yugoslavia]. Prishtinë: Enti i Teksteve dhe i Mjeteve Mësimore, 1984.

Schnytzer, Adi. *Stalinist Economic Strategy in Practice: The Case of Albania*. New York: Oxford University Press, 1982.

Shehu, Mehmet. *Raport mbi planin VII pesëvjeçar (1981–1985)* [Report on the Seventh Five-Year Plan (1981–1985)]. Tiranë: "8 Nëntori," 1981.

_____. *Vepra të zgjedhura* [Selected Works]. 1 vol. Tiranë: "8 Nëntori," 1981.

Singleton, F. B. "Albania and her Neighbours: The End of Isolation." *The World Today* 31, no. 9 (September 1975), pp. 383–90.

Sinishta, Gjon. *The Fulfilled Promise: A Documentary Account of Religious Persecution in Albania*. Santa Clara, Calif.: H and F Composing Service Printing, 1976.

Skendi, Stavro, ed. *Albania*. New York: Praeger, 1956.

_____. *Balkan Cultural Studies*. Boulder, Colo.: East European Monographs, 1980; distributed by Columbia University Press.

Thomas, John E. *Education for Communism: School and State in the People's Republic of Albania*. Stanford, Calif.: Hoover Institution Press, 1969.

Tönnes, Berhard. "Religious Persecution in Albania." *Religion in Communist Lands* 10, no. 3 (Winter 1982), pp. 242–55.

Tucoviq, Dimitrije. *Sërbia e Shqipëria* [Serbia and Albania]. Prishtinë: Rilindja, 1975.

Index

ACP. *See* Albanian Communist party
Adrian's Kingdom, 11
Adriatic Sea, 3, 4, 90, 97
Aegean Sea, 99
Afghanistan, 88, 90
Africa, 90
Agolli, Dritero, 46
Agriculture, 4, 62, 69, 79, 101
  agrarian reform, 19
  collective farms, 69–70, 76
Agron, King, 11
Air France, 101
Albanian Academy of Sciences, 29,
  41, 74, 81
Albanian Communist party (ACP),
  15, 17, 19–20, 115. *See also*
  Albanian Party of Labor
Albanian Democratic Front, 41, 59,
  61
Albanian League, 12
Albanian National Liberation Army,
  18, 115
Albanian National Liberation Front,
  18, 38, 61
Albanian Party of Labor (APL), 1,
  21–23, 30, 37, 39, 43, 53, 62,
  70, 72–73, 82–83, 87, 89, 117
  First Congress, 21, 38
  Third Congress, 40
  Fourth Congress, 38
  Sixth Congress, 26
  Seventh Congress, 28, 35, 40
  Eighth Congress, 36–37, 41, 55–56
  general line of, 2, 25, 35, 46, 51–
    53, 55, 58, 60, 65
  membership of, 55–56
  Politburo of, 40, 55–60, 78
  Secretariat, 55–57
Albanian (language), 8, 113, 118, 121
Albanoi, 11
Alia, Ramiz, 2, 10, 33–34, 36, 59,
  64, 111
  accession to power, 1, 15, 37–42
  economic policies, 48, 72–83
  foreign policy, 43–44, 88–93, 100,
    102–103
  opposition to, 2, 48–49, 80–83
  politics under, 43–49, 56–61
  and reforms, 49, 52–53, 74–83
Ali Pasha, 12
Alps, 3, 4
Amnesty International, 51
Ankara, 99
APL. *See* Albanian Party of Labor
Armed forces, 23, 25–26, 35, 51, 58
Asia, 90. *See also individual countries*
Asllani, Muho, 41, 57
Athens, 19, 89, 98–99
Aurelian, 11
Austria, 89

Bajra, Ismail, 127
Bakalli, Mahmut, 122, 124

Balkan Foreign Ministers
Conferences, 44, 93–94, 96
Balkans, 10–12, 20–22, 26, 68, 90,
92, 94–95, 98, 112
Balli Kombëtar (The National Front),
18–19
Balluku, Beqir, 22, 34–37, 54
Bar, 115
Bardhi, Jovan, 60
Bavaria, 101
Baylet, Jean-Michel, 100
Beijing, 24–28, 70, 88. *See also*
China, People's Republic of
Bekteshi, Besnik, 41–42, 57, 60
Belgrade, 19–21, 26, 54, 87, 89, 92,
94–96, 98, 99, 113, 116–117, 119,
121, 124–126, 128–129, 131–132
Belishova, Liri, 54
Beqja, Hamit, 48, 63
Berat, 10, 12
Birch, Julian, 86
Birth rate, 5, 8, 109–110
Bonn, 101
Brussels, 16
Bujan, 114
Bujan Resolution, 114–115
Bulgaria, 2, 8, 11, 92, 103
Bushati, 12
Byzantium, 11

Çako, Hito, 35
Çamëria, 12
Çami, Foto, 41–42, 48–49, 57, 81–82,
93, 97
Canada, 101
Çarçani, Adil, 36–37, 40, 42, 57, 59–
60, 81, 100
Ceausescu, Nicolae, 104
Çelaj, Zenun, 119
Çeliku, Hajredin, 41–42, 57, 60
Censorship, 29, 46
Çërava, Vangjel, 42, 57
Chetnic, 115
China, People's Republic of (PRC), 1,
23, 26–28, 34, 38, 53, 67, 70,
85, 87–88, 90–91, 103, 109

and aid to Albania, 2, 24, 26–27,
36, 67, 86, 88
Chinese Communist party, 85
Claudius II, 11
Climate, 4
CMEA. *See* Council of Mutual
Economic Assistance
Collectivization, 25, 69–70, 72
Cominform, 21
Comintern, 17
Committee of National Salvation, 18
Common Market, 26
Communications, 3
Conference on Security and
Cooperation in Europe (CSCE),
51, 87
Constantine the Great, 11
Constitution, 19, 27, 30, 35, 58–60,
86, 102
Corfu, 99
Corti, Bruno, 100
Council of Mutual Economic
Assistance (CMEA), 21, 23, 88,
91, 103
Craxi, Bettino, 100
Croatia, 108–110
CSCE. *See* Conference on Security
and Cooperation in Europe
Čubrilović, Vaso, 113
Çuko, Lenka, 41, 57
Cultural Revolution, 24–25
Culture, 10, 29, 46–47, 53
Czechoslovakia, 2, 25–27, 88, 95,
103, 121

Dalmatia, 11
Decentralization, 44, 52, 65, 70, 76–
77, 80, 82
Delo (newspaper), 96
Democratic League of Kosovë, 130
Deng Xiaoping, 28
De-Stalinization, 22–23, 54
Deva, Veli, 122
Development Assistance Committee
(DAC), 101
Devoll, 4

Dibër, 40, 116
Dinaric, 3
Diocletian, 11
Djerdja, Josip, 20
Djilas, Milovan, 20, 116
Dresden, 114
Drin River, 4
Drita (newspaper), 46
Dukagjin, 11, 114–115
Dume, Petrit, 35
Durrës, 5, 11, 13, 89
Dushan, Stephan, 11

East Berlin, 103
Eastern Europe, 1, 2, 21, 23–24, 44,
    49, 51–52, 60, 90, 103–104, 108
East Germany, 2, 103
Economy, 1, 2, 44, 46
    economic reforms, 35, 65
    Eighth Five-Year Plan (1986–1990),
        70–71, 76
    industrialization, 17, 21, 29, 67–68,
        72–73, 79
    planning, 42, 72–76, 83
    private enterprise, 58
    Seventh Five-Year Plan (1981–
        1985), 36, 69, 71
Education, 10, 25, 29, 72
Elbasan, 5
Elections, 52, 59, 64
Elezi, Mehmet, 64
Energy, 4, 29, 68, 70

Fier, 5
Fierzë, 68, 96
Fischer, Oskar, 103
Foresty, 3
France, 16–17, 100
French Communist party, 16

Gegprifti, Llambi, 40, 57
Gegs, 9
Genscher, Hans-Dietrich, 101
Geography, 3–5
Gjinushi, Skendër, 60
Gjirokastër, 5, 10, 16, 40, 89

Gjyzari, Niko, 60, 71
Gorbachev, Mikhail, 52, 103–104
Gorica, 116
Gostivar, 126
Goths, 11
Gradeci, Sulo, 16
Great Britain, 19–20, 37, 55, 102, 115
Greece, 3, 8, 12–13, 19, 26, 44–45,
    85, 88–90, 92, 94, 97–99
Greeks, 5, 98

Halili, Enver, 60
Hamza, Xhevdet, 127
Hazbiu, Kadri, 34, 36, 38, 42, 59
Health, 5, 72
Helsinki, 87
Hilmia, Sabah, 77
History, 10–13
    ancient, 10–11
    19th century, 12
    20th century, 12–13
Hoxha, Enver, 1, 10, 15, 33, 38–41,
    44–45, 47–48, 52, 55, 112, 115
    accession to power, 16–19
    and cult of personality, 22
    economic policies, 28–30, 34–35,
        68–69, 74–76, 80
    foreign policy, 1, 26–27, 85–87,
        90–94, 99–100
    politics under, 19–31, 51–54, 58
    and Stalinism, 22–23
Hoxha, Fadil, 114, 116, 127
Hoxha, Farudin, 60
Hoxha, Hysen, 16
Hoxha, Mehmet, 120
Hoxha, Nexhmije, 10, 37, 41, 61
Hua Guofeng, 28
Human rights, 30, 43, 45–47, 49, 59,
    90, 97–98, 100–101, 104
L'Humanité (newspaper), 16
Hungary, 2, 22–23, 103
Huns, 11
Hydroelectric power, 4, 68

Illiteracy, 10, 13, 17, 29
Illyrian Kingdom, 10

Illyrians, 10–11
Independence, 12, 113
Institute of Albanological Studies,
    126
Intifada, 132
Intellectuals. *See* Intelligentsia
Intelligentsia, 43, 46
Ionian Sea, 3
Isai, Hekuran, 40–41, 57
Islami, Hivzi, 119
Isolationism, 1, 27–31, 42–44, 85,
    87–88, 91–94
Italy, 3, 8, 13, 17–18, 44, 85, 89–92,
    99–100, 104

Jakova, Tuk, 22, 54
Janina, 12
Japan, 101
Jashari, Kaçusha, 107
Justinian, 11

Kadare, Ismail, 47
Kakavija, 89
Kamberi, Ahmet, 60
Kampuchea, 90
Kapllani, Muhamet, 93
Kapo, Hysni, 22, 34, 36–38, 60
Kapo, Vito, 60
Kardelj, Edvard, 116
Këllezi, Abdyl, 35, 40, 54
Kelmendi, Ramiz, 128
Khrushchev, Nikita S., 22–23, 38, 52,
    91
Koçollari, Sotir, 62
Koli, Robert, 77
Koman, 68
Kondi, Pirro, 42, 57
Korbeci, Shane, 60
Korçë, 5, 10, 16, 46
Kosovë, 5, 9–10, 13, 18–19, 44, 85,
    88, 92, 105
  Albania's position on, 94–98, 104,
    111
  demonstrations in, 107–108, 121,
    124–125, 127–130
  economic and social conditions,
    109–111, 119–120, 123, 125–126

historical background of, 112–114
persecution of Albanians, 107–109,
    115–119, 123–125, 129, 131
population of, 109–110, 122–125
republic, demands for, 116, 120–
    123, 130–131
self-determination, calls for, 114–
    116, 120
Serbs and Montenegrins in, 109,
    111–112, 114, 117, 121–123, 126–
    127
Kosovë League of Communists, 111
Kosovë-Metohija (Kosmet), 116
Kremlin. *See* Soviet Union
Krujë, 41
Kumanovë, 126

Latin America, 90
Lazri, Sofokli, 92
League of Nations, 13
Lebanon, 128
Legaliteti (Legality), 18
Lenin, V. I., Higher Party School, 37,
    56
Librazhd, 40, 73
Literature, 46–47
Ljubljana, 96–97
Lleshi, Haxhi, 37
Logoreci, Anton, 133n
London, 102
London Conference (1913), 12
Lubonja, Todi, 34
Lushnje, 41
  Congress of (1920), 13

Macedonia, 109–111, 115–117, 125,
    129
  Albanians in, 5, 9, 111, 121, 126,
    128–130
Malëshova, Sejfulla, 19–20
Malile, Reis, 60, 94, 96, 101
Mao Zedong, 25, 27–28, 36
Mara, Hekuran, 74
Marko, Rita, 40, 42, 57
Marmullaku, Ramadan, 15
Marxism. *See* Marxism-Leninism

Marxism-Leninism, 2, 15, 17, 24, 26, 35, 39, 43, 52–54, 63, 81, 85–86, 90, 93, 104, 114
Mass media, 29, 46, 48, 58, 63, 73, 78, 88, 92, 103–104
Mediterranean Sea, 4
Mero, Agim, 34
Middle East, 90
Mihali, Qirjako, 40, 57
Mikoyan, Anastas I., 34
Milliez, Paul, 38
Milošević, Slobodan, 107–109, 127–128, 131
Mineral resources, 68, 70–71
Minnesota Lawyers International Human Rights Committee, 51–52
Miska, Pali, 40–41, 57, 59
Mitrovicę, 107
Montenegro, 12–13, 109–111, 115–117, 129
    Albanians in, 5, 9–10, 121, 126, 130
Morina, Rrahman, 108
Moscow, 21–24, 38, 87, 90–91, 103, 115. See also Soviet Union
Mother Teresa, 10
Mugoša, Dušan, 17–18
Murati, Osman, 60
Murra, Prokop, 41–42, 57, 60
Mustaqi, Kiço, 42, 57
Muzakas, 11
Myftiu, Manush, 40, 42, 57, 59

Nako, Andrea, 60, 73
Nase, Nesti, 37–38
NATO. See North Atlantic Treaty Organization
Ngjela, Kiço, 35
Nimani, Xhavit, 127
Nixon, Richard M., 26–27
NLF. See Albanian National Liberation Front
Normans, 11
North Atlantic Treaty Organization (NATO), 3, 26, 90, 92

OECD. See Organization for Economic Cooperation and Development
Oil industry, 4, 29, 41, 70–71, 89, 91, 102
Organization for Economic Cooperation and Development (OECD), 101
Osum River, 4
Ottoman Empire, 10, 13, 112

Paçrami, Fadil, 34
Pano, Nicholas C., 52
Papandreou, Andreas, 98–99
Papoulias, Karolos, 99
Paris, 101
    Conference of (1919), 13
Pasha, Ali, 12
Pejë (Peć), 112
Permet, 41
Plaka, Sokrat, 89
Pogradec, 4
Poland, 2, 22–23, 80
Popović, Miladin, 17–18, 116
Population, 5, 8
Pravda (newspaper), 91
PRC. See China, People's Republic of
Prespë, 3, 4
Prifti, Peter R., 16
Prishtinë, 96, 107–108, 121, 126, 128–129
Private property, 72–76, 80
Prizren, 12, 96
    League of (1878), 12
Probus, 11
Progon, 11
Pula, Imer, 127

Qemal, Ismail, 12
Qosja, Rexhep, 96, 126, 128–129

Rajević, Radošin, 113
Ranković, Aleksandar, 116, 118, 120, 127, 131
Religion, 10, 25, 43, 45, 58
Rexha, Lumturie, 61

Rilindja (newspaper), 108
Roman Empire, 11
Romania, 2, 8, 26, 28, 92, 104, 109
Rome, 11, 13, 89, 100
Rruga e Partisë (journal), 77–78, 102
Rugova, Ibrahim, 130

São Paulo, 96
Sarandë, 5, 99
Secret police (Sigurimi), 2, 19, 34,
    47, 51
Self-reliance, 27, 35, 53, 67, 70, 82,
    86, 102, 104
Seman, 4
Serbia, 12–13, 104, 107, 109–110,
    112, 116, 120, 122, 126–127,
    129–131
Serbian Empire, 11
Serbian Patriarchate, 112
Serbo-Croat (language), 20, 118, 121
Serbs, 11, 20, 115, 120, 131. *See also*
    Kosovë
Shala, Rezhak, 121
Shehu, Feçor, 36–37, 59
Shehu, Fiqret, 37–38
Shehu, Mehmet, 22, 33–38, 42, 55,
    59, 74, 87
Shkodër, 3–5, 12, 38, 41, 88, 91, 98
Shkreli, Azem, 128
Shkumbin, 4, 9
Shpata, 11
Shqipëri, 11
Sigurimi. See Secret police
Skënderbeu, Gjergj Kastrioti, 11–12
Skendi, Stavro, 13
Slavs, 5, 11, 20, 109, 113, 131
Slovenia, 108–110
Soviet Communist Party, 22–23, 52
Soviet Union, 1, 17–18, 20–26, 28,
    33–34, 37–38, 40, 52–53, 55, 67,
    85–88, 90, 92, 95, 103–105, 109,
    115, 117, 121
Spahiu, Bedri, 22, 54
Spiru, Nako, 21
Stalin, Joseph, 17, 21, 34, 39, 52,
    108, 117

Stalinism, 1, 2, 29, 39, 51, 52, 67,
    72, 82, 90
Standard of living, 2, 17, 44, 67, 75,
    83
Stefani, Simon, 41, 57, 59, 73
Strauss, Franz-Josef, 101
Swissair, 101

Tafaj, Xhemal, 60
Taiwan, 25
Tashko, Koço, 54
Taxes, 29
Technology, 31, 70, 89, 91, 92, 100–
    102, 104
Teheran, 114
Tempo, Svetozar Vukmanović, 116
Tetovë, 115–116
Theodhosi, Koço, 35, 40, 54
Thessaly, 12
Thikat (novel), 47
Third World, 23, 26, 28, 44, 83, 87,
    123
Tiranë, 5, 10, 16, 19–20, 22–23, 25–
    26, 28, 41, 45–46, 52, 54, 58,
    67, 81, 87–91, 94, 96, 98–104,
    117, 119, 121, 128
Tito, Josip B., 22–23, 28, 94, 99, 107,
    115, 117, 121
Titograd, 88, 98
Tokyo, 96
Topias, 11
Tosks, 9
Tourism, 45
Tozaj, Neshat, 45
Trieste, 89, 116
Tropojë, 88
Turkey, 8, 44, 88–89, 92, 98–99,
    113–114
Turks, 11–12

Uçi, Alfred, 60
Union of Albanian Women, 61
Union of Albanian Working Youth,
    37, 62–64
Union of Albanian Writers and
    Artists, 29, 46

United Nations, 20, 24, 46, 90, 94
United Trade Unions, 62, 104
United States, 3, 10, 16, 19–20, 23–
      27, 37, 55, 86, 87, 90, 92, 104,
      112, 115
USSR. *See* Soviet Union

Vietnam, 25
Vjosa, 4
Vllasi, Azem, 107–108, 127–129
Vlorë, 5, 10, 12
Vojvodina, 107, 109–110, 116–117,
      127

Warsaw Treaty Organization, 21, 23,
      25, 88, 91–92, 103
Washington, 26, 87
Western Europe, 26–28, 45, 70, 87–
      90, 98–100, 103, 111–112
West Germany, 44, 100–102, 104
Wied, Wilhelm zu, 13
Women, 25, 30, 55, 61–62

World Court, 101

Xoxe, Koçi, 18–22, 54

YCP. *See* Yugoslav Communist party
YLC. *See* Yugoslav League of
      Communists
Ylli, Ajet, 60
Youth, 2, 43, 62–64
Yugoslav Communist party, 17, 18,
      20, 114
Yugoslavia, 1, 3, 20, 21–23, 26, 28,
      34, 37–38, 44–45, 54–55, 67–68,
      80, 85, 87–98, 105, 111, 114,
      128–132
Yugoslav League of Communists,
      122–123

Zagreb, 114
Zëri i Popullit (newspaper), 48, 79
Ziçishti, Llambi, 37–38
Zog, King Ahmet, 13, 16, 18, 67
Zogu. *See* Zog, King Ahmet